"*Conquer Your Critical Inner Voice* presents a wise, bold, and provocative alternative to the limits of similar self-help books. The chapter on intimacy and couple relationships alone is worth the price of the book. Complex psychological phenomena are described in concrete and clear language. The authors offer numerous exercises to help the reader put the book's ideas to immediate use, and they include guidelines for therapists who may want to use the book in their work with patients in psychotherapy."

—Charles Bonner, Ph.D., Clinical Psychologist, private practice, Pittsburgh, PA

"As a psychologist, spouse, and parent, I have been influenced by the wisdom inherent in the work of *Conquer Your Critical Inner Voice*. The authors convey to the reader in simple terms the relevancy of their profound psychology. I am inspired by their commitment to help readers liberate themselves from a legacy that undermines their essential well-being and right to a life."

—Richard Vogel, Ph.D., coauthor of *Brief Psychotherapy Methods,* associate of Weiss-Sampson Control Mastery Theory Group, San Francisco

"I am very pleased that this book is being published because it contains information invaluable to individuals and families. We tend to express our deepest self-feelings in an interior voice that is at times heavily infused with self-critical messages. For many, these negative messages inhibit productive activity and success in relationships. The authors provide a series of self-help exercises to aid in overcoming the painful distances in relationships with those they love and care about."

—Gail McCracken Price, Ph.D., Clinical Psychologist, Radcliffe Seminars Adjunct Faculty

conquer your
critical
inner
voice

**A REVOLUTIONARY PROGRAM TO COUNTER NEGATIVE THOUGHTS
AND LIVE FREE FROM IMAGINED LIMITATIONS**

**Robert W. Firestone, Ph.D. • Lisa Firestone, Ph.D.
Joyce Catlett, M.A.**

FOREWORD BY PAT LOVE, ED.D.

NEW HARBINGER PUBLICATIONS, INC.

Publisher's Note

Distributed in Canada by Raincoast Books

Copyright © 2002 by Robert W. Firestone, Lisa Firestone, and Joyce Catlett
New Harbinger Publications, Inc.
5674 Shattuck Avenue
Oakland, CA 94609

Cover design by Salmon Studios
Edited by Clancy Drake
Text design by Tracy Marie Carlson

ISBN-10 1-57224-287-6
ISBN-13 978-1-57224-287-6

Printed in the United States of America

New Harbinger Publications' website address: www.newharbinger.com

16   15   14

15   14   13   12   11   10

We would like to dedicate this book to our coauthor Robert Firestone, whose inspirational ideas have impacted our lives and the lives of the many people with whom we have shared them through lectures and presentations over the past twenty years. The personal responses of our audiences motivated us to convince him to write a book with us that would make these ideas more accessible to the general reader. We wish to express our appreciation for, and admiration of, the courage with which Robert Firestone has continuously exposed the destructiveness of psychological defenses and challenged conventional beliefs both in the field of psychology and in the larger society.

—Lisa Firestone and Joyce Catlett

Contents

Part I
Understanding Your Critical Inner Voice

Part II
Challenging The Critical Inner Voice

Acknowledgments

We are especially grateful to Tamsen Firestone for her unusual sensitivity and insight in organizing, rewriting, and clarifying the ideas contained in this book. We also extend our thanks to her team of outstanding editors, Jo Barrington and Susan Short, for their continuing critique and evaluation of the manuscript; to Anne Baker for her help in completing the final draft; to Tracy Larkin and Sara Hoopes for reproducing the exercises; and to Jina Carvalho for disseminating an expanding body of written and filmed works that elucidate these concepts and methods.

We also thank Matthew McKay for encouraging us to write this book We particularly want to express our gratitude to the men and women whose stories gave life to the ideas and methods described in this book. We want to thank them for their openness and honesty in revealing their personal truths and contributing to the pool of knowledge about the critical inner voice and the fantasy bond.

Foreword

Are you living the good life—the life of your dreams? If so, no doubt you are following the principles outlined in this book. But if you are frequently met with disappointment, even discouragement, take heart, because this book is written for you. Within its pages lies a powerful program that will take you step by step into awareness of the inner critical voice that is controlling your life and stifling your energy. It will reveal how and why you fall short of your capabilities and give you clear guidelines for correcting the habits that have limited you for so long.

Reading this book had a powerful impact on me. Even though I've been a therapist, researcher, author, and trainer for more than twenty years, I too struggle with my inner critical voice. The protean monster has taken many forms, such as depression, anxiety, overworking, relationship struggles, vanity, lethargy, and mind-numbing habits like losing myself in old movies and e-mail. To my surprise, this book quickly blew the cover on all these defenses and compassionately exposed my critical inner voice as the enemy. As I followed the exercises, I could feel my mood lift, my spirits rise, and my outlook become more hopeful. This experience led me to the conclusion that most of all, this is a book of hope. It kindly describes the human dilemma; explains the origins of the critical inner voice in a nonblaming way; and most important, it gives user-friendly steps to free us of our limitations.

You, the Reader, stand to gain a great deal from your journey through this book. It provides an opportunity for you to come face to face with your internal enemy and acknowledge the fact that you—like many of us—tend to underestimate the extent to which hostile thoughts control your life. You can gain new insight about why you may be falling far below your capabilities in your work, as well as in your love life. (I especially liked the section on relationships, and the graphic describing the six qualities to look for in an ideal partner is worth the price of the book!)

Finally, one piece of advice—take your time with the program outlined here before you. I found that reading a chapter, then working the exercises, then going back over the chapter was a very helpful process. If you follow the guidelines as suggested, I believe you will be comforted by the realization that this program can and will counter your negative thoughts. The internal enemy will no longer be able to hide and sabotage your success, and ultimately you will become acquainted with the Real You—the friendly, compassionate person you were designed to be. I know this is a tall order, but my experience says this book can deliver.

—Pat Love, Ed.D.
Relationship consultant and author of
The Truth About Love

Introduction

Our life is what our thoughts make it.

—Marcus Aurelius

This book poses a number of important questions: "Whose life are you really living?" "Are you pursuing your life as a fully vital human being, or are you unintentionally living a life prescribed by others?" "Are you truly following your own destiny, or are you repeating the life of your parents?" It is crucial for every person to seriously consider these questions. It is valuable to become aware of what you are telling yourself and to discover the negative prescriptions by which you may be living your life. It is beneficial, although understandably painful, to realize that, like all people, you are divided within—that you are under attack, in a sense, by an internal enemy. This kind of awareness can free you and set into motion the process of change.

The goal of this book is to provide you with the insights gained during twenty-five years of investigations into the critical inner voice. *Conquer Your Critical Inner Voice* offers a means by which readers can free themselves from the harmful effects of this destructive process. The more people recognize that they do have an enemy within, the greater the opportunity they have for overcoming its negative effects on their lives. The guidelines and exercises provided in this book point you toward leading a better life by identifying the critical inner voice, understanding its sources, and then taking action against its dictates. The personal stories of the many men and women who took part in these studies demonstrate how you can use this information to further your personal development, find more satisfaction in your relationships, and achieve success in your chosen career.

This book focuses on understanding all aspects of our critical inner voice, including the emotions associated with it and the many ways in which it impacts each area of our daily lives. The chapters outline methods to identify and counteract the voice's profound influence so that you can live a more fulfilling life, develop your own ideals, values, and priorities, and embark on your own search for meaning in life. The suggestions, guidelines, and techniques described throughout this volume are based on the methods of *voice therapy*, which was developed by Dr. Robert Firestone, clinical psychologist and author or coauthor of *The Fantasy Bond* (1985), *Voice Therapy* (1988), *Compassionate Child-Rearing* (1990), *Psychological Defenses in Everyday Life* (1989, with Joyce Catlett), *Combating Destructive Thought Processes* (1997a), *Suicide and the Inner Voice* (1997b), and *Fear of Intimacy* (1999, with Joyce Catlett).

Organization of This Book

This book is divided into three parts. Part I, "Understanding Your Critical Inner Voice," describes the everyday self-critical and hostile voices that people are most familiar with. These operate on a more conscious level and are virtually universal. Chapter 1 explains where these voices come from—how they are originally formed and then reinforced throughout childhood. Sample journal pages are provided that can be helpful in identifying these negative thoughts and separating them from a more realistic and compassionate point of view toward yourself. Chapter 2 describes how the inner voice diminishes our self-esteem, makes us feel ashamed about imagined or real deficiencies, and restricts our life experience by promoting guilt reactions. This chapter offers suggestions and exercises to help alleviate feelings of guilt and shame by identifying the underlying voices.

Each chapter in part II, "Challenging the Critical Inner Voice," outlines specific negative thoughts or voices that interfere with your achieving your goals in a particular area of your life. They describe what your critical inner voice may be telling you in the myriad of situations that arise in the course of everyday living. The chapters also provide guidelines and exercises for counteracting these voices and changing behaviors controlled by them.

Chapter 3 identifies negative thoughts that contribute to nonproductive ways of working, explains why many people react adversely to success, and provides suggestions for remedying these behaviors and developing good work habits. Chapter 4 illuminates the voices that cause distress in our closest, most intimate relationships. It explains how the inner voice acts to preserve an illusion of love at the expense of genuine love and closeness. Chapter 5 shows how almost every person in our culture is damaged incidentally by family, peer, and societal attitudes toward sex and the human body. It provides exercises that couples can use to identify the negative voices about their sexuality that interfere with intimacy and thus recapture feelings of sexual desire and closeness.

Chapter 6 reveals the voices underlying various forms of self-defeating behaviors, with an emphasis on the thought patterns that are involved in addictive behaviors. Methods for identifying and countering the contradictory voices of addiction will be described. Chapter 7 addresses the problem of depression. It identifies a continuum of self-destructive thoughts ranging from those that merely limit our lives to thoughts that influence us to engage in seriously self-destructive behaviors. Exercises help you identify the negative thoughts that contribute to depression and the feelings aroused by these thoughts, and give suggestions for changing the behaviors influenced by these thoughts.

Chapter 8 discusses the characteristics to look for in a therapist or counselor and provides guidelines for how to find a good therapist. This information is offered in case you wish to further pursue your own personal development or feel that you could benefit from professional help with a particular area of your life.

In part III, "Guidelines for Living the 'Good Life'," chapter 9 provides parents with an understanding of how the critical inner voice is formed early in life and how our society unfortunately supports this negative way of thinking in children. Nothing is more important to the future than our children; therefore this chapter provides guidelines and suggestions to help parents develop more positive, compassionate attitudes toward themselves, which will then allow them to have a positive effect on their children.

Chapter 10 describes an ongoing lifelong journey of self-discovery that many people embark on as they continue to identify, challenge, and go against the dictates of their critical inner voice. To supplement the methods, suggestions, and exercises in previous chapters, the authors delineate additional steps developed by Robert Firestone that you can take to move toward achieving a more fulfilling life. An understanding of the internal and external forces in life that are confining, toxic, and demoralizing has led Dr. Firestone to formulate ideas (to be published in his forthcoming book *The Good Life*) about the types of experiences that would be conducive to a person's well-being and personal growth. This chapter points out the importance of friendship, generosity, developing your own value system, taking risks in being more vulnerable in relationships, and learning to face painful existential issues without defending yourself.

Conquer Your Critical Inner Voice can help you expose and challenge destructive ways of thinking that seriously impair your sense of self, your spirit, and your ability to achieve the things in life that matter the most to you. Many limitations that people face in life are self-imposed and based on unrealistic and negative views they have of themselves and others. Therefore, the goals of this book are: (1) to illuminate the forces within us that contribute to many of our problems in living and that cause us much unnecessary pain and distress; and (2) to provide you with methods for challenging and modifying these forces so you can realize your own unique potentialities.

A Note to Therapists

Voice therapy methods can be used as an adjunct to cognitive behavioral, psychodynamic, and existential/humanistic psychotherapies. If you are interested in becoming familiar with the steps in the therapeutic process using voice therapy and gaining a broader understanding of the underlying theory, you may want to read *Voice Therapy: A Psychotherapeutic Approach to Self-Destructive Behavior* (Firestone 1988), *Combating Destructive Thought Processes* (Firestone 1997a), *Suicide and the Inner Voice* (Firestone 1997b), and *Fear of Intimacy* (Firestone and Catlett 1999). In addition, you may want to view the voice therapy training videos, which illustrate the methods with real individuals. *A Voice Therapy Training Manual* (Firestone, Firestone, and Catlett 1997), and all of the materials mentioned in this paragraph are available from the Glendon Association, 5383 Hollister Ave. No. 230, Santa Barbara, CA 93111. Information regarding training seminars in voice therapy can also be found on this Web site, www.glendon.org.

Cognitive Behavioral Therapists

This book may be used as a valuable addition to cognitive behavioral treatment. Clients' negative thoughts toward self that they record in their journals can be brought into the sessions and addressed directly. The exercises can be used as homework assignments, and can become an important part of the therapeutic process. The various questionnaires containing negative self-statements can directly encourage clients to bring up in the session important subject matter or material they have not previously addressed. The exercises and questionnaires can facilitate a process of investigation in clients regarding the connection between cognitions, affect, and behavior. The methods of journaling with the divided page format can help clients examine the evidence for and against their distorted, automatic, negative thoughts by using reality testing, setting goals, and taking corrective actions toward those goals. The journaling format also helps them develop insight and institute behavior changes in a way that can be integrated into CBT to challenge the reality of the critical inner voice.

The methods of voice therapy bring to the surface not only negative or dysfunctional cognitions but also the feelings associated with them. Identifying "automatic thoughts" in the presence of strong affect can provide the "hot emotional climate" necessary for changing core schemas.

Psychodynamic Psychoanalytic Therapists

For psychodynamic therapists, this book describes how early object relations impact later development and personality dynamics. It provides methods (exercises, questionnaires, and journaling techniques) for accessing "negative parental introjects" or, in terms of attachment theory, "internal working models" that may have been defensively excluded from the client's conscious awareness. The personal stories, examples, and journaling exercises can provide the client insight into partially unconscious processes, and can give the therapist access to clinical data similar to information obtained through the technique of free association. This material can provide insight into how internal working models or representations are manifested in the client's current life.

Voice therapy techniques could be used to provide clinicians with an in-depth understanding of the parental environment of their clients. We have found that the exercises tend to lead to clients' raising issues that they may not have previously addressed in treatment. In addition, understanding the client's transference as an attempt to reenact the rejection he or she experienced in his or her family of origin can be helpful to clinicians in conceptualizing the client's personality dynamics and in developing interpretations. For example, specific items of the questionnaires that predict rejection or negative consequences may be endorsed with high frequency by clients manifesting negative transference reactions.

Existential Humanistic Therapists

Therapists working within an existential or humanistic framework may be particularly interested in negative thoughts the client endorses that are related to guilt, self-denial, isolation, hopelessness, and giving up. Understanding that people suffer death anxiety in relation to positive as well as negative events in life, existential therapists could inquire about events (both positive and negative) that may have precipitated a negative therapeutic reaction or the acting out of self-destructive behavior in a client. Reading this book will help clients better understand existential issues of aloneness and death and how they form defenses against death anxiety. In addition, chapter 10 may encourage clients to embrace life in spite of death and to use their awareness of a finite existence to enhance rather than give up on their lives.

Part I

Understanding Your Critical Inner Voice

Part I focuses on the self-critical voices and hostile, cynical thoughts toward others that people are the most aware of in their everyday lives. These critical inner voices usually exist on a conscious level and are among the most common ones experienced by people from many different backgrounds and cultures. These negative thoughts originate in childhood and persist into adult life. The chapters focus on how the critical inner voice decreases your self-esteem and limits your ability to fulfill yourself in life by making you feel ashamed and guilty. The exercises are designed to help you identify these destructive thoughts, the events that trigger them, and the behaviors they influence. Several techniques are also suggested to counter the effects of the critical inner voice and increase your feelings of self-worth and self-esteem.

Chapter 1

Becoming Familiar with Your Critical Inner Voice

We allow ourselves to be ruled and controlled by our thoughts and emotions, and furthermore . . . we allow our thoughts and emotions to be determined by our negative impulses and other afflictions of the mind. . . . If we continue to allow this situation to occur, it can only lead to misery and suffering. . . . Whatever brings disaster or harm should be called an enemy, so this means that the ultimate enemy is actually within ourselves.

—The Fourteenth Dalai Lama

A man about to give a speech thinks: *"You're going to make a fool of yourself. You're going to sound stupid. They're all going to laugh at you. Who wants to listen to what you have to say, anyway?"*

A woman preparing to go on a date tells herself: *"What makes you think he'll like you? You'd better think of something interesting to talk about or he won't call again."*

A young man applying for a job thinks: *"You're too young and inexperienced for this job. Why even bother writing a resume? You're never going to get a job like this anyway."*

A child taking a test at school is distracted by thoughts like: *"You're such an idiot! You can't do anything right. You're going to fail this test."*

Do you ever have thoughts like these? What effect do they have on your life? How do they make you feel when you experience them? By becoming aware of these types of thoughts and how they affect your actions and emotions, you can take more control over your life. Becoming familiar with every aspect of the critical inner voice can help you bring your actions more in line with your real goals in life.

How Your Critical Inner Voice Controls Your Actions

Why did the man giving the speech berate himself in a way that actually increased his nervousness? Why did the young man envision failure in finding a job? Why did these people perceive these situations in a negative light and make predictions about the future in a way that had a detrimental effect on their feelings and their behavior?

Destructive thoughts such as these strongly influence our actions and the way we conduct our daily lives. For example, the man giving the speech did stumble over his words, and the man who put off writing a resume did not get the job he wanted.

Like the man giving the speech, we are all aware of thoughts that increase our nervousness and interfere with our performance. However, most of us tend to underestimate the extent to which these hostile thoughts are directing our lives. The sneering, belittling self-criticisms described in the examples above are only the tip of the iceberg in terms of the underlying anger we feel toward ourselves. They are merely the more visible fragments of a larger, well-hidden enemy within, a powerful adversary made up of destructive thoughts, beliefs, and attitudes that control our actions, interfere with the pursuit of our personal and career goals, and make us feel bad a good deal of the time.

Do you have this type of inner enemy? This chapter will help you to identify the critical voice within yourself and discover the many ways that it impacts your life. This knowledge is the first step in conquering your critical inner voice.

Being for Yourself or Against Yourself

All of us are divided within ourselves and have a basic conflict in relation to our goals and aspirations in life. On one hand, we have feelings of warm self-regard, and we have traits and behaviors that we like or feel comfortable with in ourselves. We have natural tendencies to grow and develop and to pursue our personal and vocational goals, as well as desires to be close in our relationships and to search for meaning in life. In this book, these tendencies are referred to as the *real you* or your *real self*, because they are made up of a friendly, compassionate view of yourself.

On the other hand, we have an unfriendly, critical view of ourselves. Often these destructive thoughts and attitudes become intense and take precedence over our more realistic or positive ways of thinking. They influence us to limit ourselves and sabotage our successes and, at times, to feel hostile and cynical toward other people. In some cases, under stressful conditions, this negative way of thinking can increase, gaining more control over our actions, and can actually lead to seriously self-destructive behavior. This negative side, as well as its critical, angry point of view, is referred to in this book as the *critical inner voice*, because it is the part of you that is turned against your real self. It encourages and strongly influences self-defeating and self-destructive behavior, and it promotes angry or hurtful attitudes toward other people as well.

Depending on which part of your personality is more prominent at a given time, the real you or the critical inner voice, you will express an entirely different point of view, and your behaviors and interactions with others will be different. Perhaps you have noticed this interesting phenomenon in the people close to you; they can be very different when they seem to be "themselves" than when they do not seem themselves. When they are themselves, they are usually relaxed and far more likable. When they are being influenced by their critical inner voice, they are typically more uptight and unlikable.

How Did You Develop a Critical Inner Voice?

How is it that we can be so turned against ourselves? Where did this enemy within come from? How did we end up with this critical inner voice? The answers lie in the past when, as children, we were trying to cope with our lives in the best way possible.

The nature and degree of this division within ourselves depends on the parenting we received and the early environment we experienced. Parents, like all of us, have mixed feelings toward themselves; they have things they like about themselves and they have self-critical thoughts and feelings. The same negative feelings that parents have toward themselves are unfortunately often directed toward their children as well. Therefore, parents have both loving feelings toward their children as well as critical thoughts and negative feelings toward them. Mothers and fathers who feel that they are bad find it difficult to believe that something good could come from them. In addition, children, just by their presence, tend to stir up in their parents the feelings they had when they were children. If a parent has unresolved feelings from either trauma or loss in his or her past, these feelings will impact his or her reactions to his or her children.

Every childhood includes situations where the child's needs are not met and, as a result, the child has feelings of frustration or suffers emotional pain. We all experienced moments of rejection, neglect, or even hostility from our parents or primary caretakers. These incidents, whether they were frequent or rare, made a significant impression on us.

Most of us, if asked, could recount in surprising detail a time when one of our parents lost control. What provoked our parent's anger is often forgotten, but the feeling from the experience is clear and lives on in our memory. We had to try to protect ourselves against the fear, anxiety, and pain that were aroused at those times when our parents, in spite of their best intentions, acted out angrily toward us, humiliated us, or were indifferent to our feelings.

Children learn to treat themselves in much the same way their parents treated them. In other words, people tend to parent themselves as they were parented, both soothing and punishing themselves in a manner similar to the ways their parents soothed and punished them.

Your Defenses

Defenses are the ways that we coped with these stressful or painful situations. As children, we developed ways of protecting ourselves in proportion to the degree of emotional pain we experienced in our families. Our defenses helped us when we were young, but now that we are adults, they limit us and interfere with our developing to our full potential. These psychological defenses can be compared to our body's physical reaction in the case of pneumonia. In this disease, our body's defensive reaction is more destructive than the original assault from the bacteria that invaded our body. The presence of bacteria in our lungs causes changes in our immune system, which sends out antibodies to meet the invasion. However, the magnitude of this defensive reaction leads to congestion that is potentially dangerous to us.

In a similar way, the defenses that we erected as small, vulnerable children to protect ourselves in painful situations may become more harmful than the original trauma we endured. In this sense, our psychological defenses become the bases for our later problems in living.

The Fantasy Bond—The First Line of Defense

Dr. Robert Firestone (1985) has found that the most powerful and basic defense that we develop as children—a defense that provides relief and security when we are suffering—is a fantasy of being connected to our mother or primary caregiver. He has labeled this defense the *fantasy bond*. Infants have a natural ability to comfort themselves by using images and memories of past feeding experiences to ward off the anxiety of being temporarily separated from their mother and to help reduce their feelings of hunger and frustration.

The power of the human imagination to relieve pain is extraordinary. For example, research studies conducted during World War II found that daydreaming and fantasizing about food actually reduced physical hunger pangs in people who were near starvation.

When parents are mostly unavailable or inconsistent in meeting their infant's needs, the infant turns more and more to an image of being connected to the parents. This fantasy, like most fantasies, becomes a substitute for real gratification. The child becomes dependent on this fantasy as a means of self-gratification. If a baby or young child were able to express this feeling of false independence, he or she might say, "I can take care of myself—I don't need anyone."

Children support this illusion of being self-sufficient with behaviors that relieve tension, such as thumb-sucking, rubbing a blanket, and, later on, behaviors that help them numb painful feelings. In fact, almost any behavior, carried to excess, can be used for this purpose. Often, we come to prefer the fantasy bond and these other ways of soothing ourselves to depending on others for fulfillment of our needs.

As infants, in the process of becoming united with our parents in our imaginations, we take in their attitudes toward us. Unfortunately, these not only include their positive attitudes, but their negative ones as well. These internalized antagonistic attitudes form the basis of the critical inner voice.

Here is an example of a child who developed a fantasy of being self-sufficient and the behaviors she used to support her fantasy.

The Story of Kayla

Kayla's parents had been married for three years when she was born. She was their first child and they were somewhat ill-equipped to take care of a new baby. They tended to be overprotective, and attempted to soothe Kayla's frequent crying by using everything they could think of—pacifiers, music, rocking her for hours—but her misery seemed endless despite their constant attention.

Kayla's mother had suffered rejection herself as a child and was nervous holding Kayla. She held her very tightly against her chest and paced the floor while bouncing her up and down in an exaggerated motion, trying to quiet her. Kayla's father was passive and indulgent; he took his cue from the mother and participated in the vigorous bouncing ritual.

When Kayla was a year old, her parents began having marital problems, and her mother was absent for long periods of time. Kayla began to become more and more agitated and distressed. It seemed that only one technique was effective in calming her: she insisted on being held by a person standing upright. She would bury her head in the person's shoulder, her body would go limp, and she would stop crying and become silent. She would lie lifeless in the person's arms like a rag doll, with her eyes partly closed and glazed over. At these times, she had the appearance of a person on drugs.

By the time she was two and a half, Kayla began showing signs of withdrawal. Often, she appeared lost in a world of her own. She had a peculiar way of playing with her toys: one of her favorite pastimes was to repeatedly stack and organize blocks, coins, or playing cards in precise piles or rows. She would scream if a playmate disturbed a stack or row of her objects. In addition, Kayla tried to avoid affectionate contact. She would grimace and actually recoil from affection.

Kayla developed a bedtime ritual that could not be varied. She demanded a specific sequence of songs, bedtime stories, and her favorite ritual—the familiar journey on either her mother's or father's shoulder with her head turned away from the world. She repeatedly requested one song or story; if another tune or story were suggested, she would stiffen her body and scream, "No! No! Same song! Same song!"

It appeared that Kayla had lost many of her natural wants and desires. Because of her parents' nervousness and agitation, Kayla had formed a fantasy of self-sufficiency and used objects and activities in a ritualized way to reinforce her illusion that she could take care of herself. When these activities were interrupted, she felt panicked because her fantasy was being threatened, and she reacted with rage. Because these rituals had relieved her early distress and partly filled her needs, she became more and more addicted to them as she got older. In essence, her real wants were transformed into a continual search for *something* to fill an emptiness within her. When she found "it," though, she was never satisfied for very long and would soon resume her search. By the time she was three years old, Kayla had become very much like an addict, and rituals and activities were her drugs.

How Learning About Death Strengthens the Fantasy Bond

Sometime between the ages of three and seven, we learn about death. This new awareness of the inevitability of death causes us deep sadness and fear and turns our whole world upside down. The things that we thought were permanent, we now realize are temporary, including our own lives. To cope with these overwhelming feelings, we rely on the same defenses we formed to deal with the emotional pain in our early environment. In this way, the defenses that we have already developed become strengthened and more ingrained in our personality.

After learning about death, many children make vows, on a deep, subconscious level, to never invest fully in their lives and to never fully attach to another person, because they know they will someday lose their life and their loved ones. We go in and out of aligning ourselves either with life—choosing to live in spite of a finite existence—or aligning ourselves with death—defending ourselves and limiting our lives in an attempt to protect ourselves against the fear of death. It is important for us to develop an awareness of whether we are siding with life or siding with death as we go through our daily lives.

Internalizing the Angry Parent—
Our Second Line of Defense

Because of their acute sensitivity to pain and negative circumstances, children of all ages pay particular attention to, and are deeply affected by, even small incidences of parental anger. They may experience a parent's anger, whether acted out or not, as being life-threatening. (Under extreme circumstances, they may be accurate in their perceptions.) In any case, children in stressful situations often feel threatened to the core of their beings and frightened for their lives.

During times of stress, when children are afraid, they stop identifying with themselves as the helpless child and instead identify with the verbally or physically punishing parent. The parent is assimilated or taken in as he or she is at that moment, when he or she is at his or her worst, not as he or she is every day. The child tends to take on the anger, fear, self-hatred—in fact, the whole complex of emotions the parent is experiencing at that time.

For example, Walter was usually easygoing and relaxed with his son, Jimmy—except when they were working on projects together. In these situations, Walter's perfectionism and critical nature would come across, even when Walter was trying to make the experience a pleasant one. In a parenting group, Walter became more aware of the problems he had run into as a parent when trying to teach his son, and talked about his critical tendencies:

> When Jimmy was really young, I would have a huge rage at him when he couldn't do something right. For example, if we were working on a model plane together and he couldn't hold the piece right or something like that, I would get impatient immediately and insist that he do it the right way. Sometimes I would lash out at him angrily, but mostly I would just walk away and leave him alone to try to figure it out for himself. I don't know how he was able to learn anything from me at all.

Jimmy grew up to be critical of himself in many areas. Although he made good grades in college and was active in sports, he attacked himself maliciously in each of these situations and particularly when he was working on a project:

> I thought about the way I'm hard on myself and how I put so much pressure on myself. In grammar school I was always terrified not to get all As. If I made even one B, I felt terrible. In sports, it's like I have to be the best or the worst, I can't be in between. I can't just be myself. If I'm playing baseball and I make an error, I just tear into myself. I think I'm such an idiot, I mean, I just sit there and call myself an idiot a hundred times. It's like I'm screaming at myself inside of my head.
>
> Whenever I'm trying to build something, I just dread getting into the project. Sometimes I get so nervous, my hands actually start shaking and I start thinking to myself: *"You're such a klutz. You're all thumbs. Why can't you do anything right? You're an idiot, a mechanical retard. Other guys don't have any trouble with this kind of work. What's the matter with you?"*

The Real You and Your Critical Inner Voice

The positive side of the division within each of us begins with the unique qualities we possess—physical abilities and attributes, temperament, certain predispositions, and natural identification with the positive traits that our parents or primary caretakers possess. Positive emotional experiences contribute to this part of ourselves, including what we learn, what we enjoy, and the experiences that facilitate our growth and development.

The Real You

The real you is the undefended part of your personality; this real self develops and grows as a result of your parents' and other concerned adults' nurturing qualities and behaviors and the love and care they direct toward you.

Exercise 1.1: Visualizing the Real You

In exercise 1.1 (at the end of this chapter), list your abilities and strong points, including the qualities that you like or admire in yourself. Also list your goals in life, both short-term and long-term, your special interests, and the activities that you particularly enjoy. For example, what people or causes are meaningful to you? What are your values and ideals? Lastly, write down where you stand in relation to fulfilling your goals.

The Critical Inner Voice

The critical inner voice is the language of the defended, negative side of your personality; the side that is opposed to your ongoing personal development. The voice is made up of a series of negative thoughts that oppose your best interests and diminish your self-esteem. These hostile, judgmental thoughts also warn you about other people and create a negative, pessimistic picture of the world. The voice is not only made up of destructive thoughts, attitudes, and beliefs, it also includes feelings of anger, rage, or grief that we all experience in conjunction with this way of thinking.

The critical inner voice exists to varying degrees in every person. It undermines our ability to interpret events realistically, triggers negative moods, and sabotages our pursuit of satisfaction and meaning in life. The voice essentially keeps us locked into our defense systems, while our healthier side (the real self) strives for freedom from the constraints of these defenses. These destructive internalized thoughts lead to a sense of alienation—a feeling of being removed from ourselves and distant from those we love. When we believe the negative interpretations of the voice and fail to challenge them—that is, when we "listen" to the voice—we tend to act in ways that have negative consequences for us.

Although most people are conscious of some aspects of this inner voice, many negative thoughts exist on an unconscious level. At times, we may be clearly aware of what our critical inner voice is telling us. However, at other times, we may be somewhat unclear about our negative thinking, and simply believe or accept a negative image of ourselves. In addition, we may not be fully aware of the destructive impact that these thoughts are having on our emotions, actions, and the way we are conducting our lives. It is important to note here that the critical inner voice we are discussing is not an auditory hallucination but instead is experienced as thoughts within your head.

The Critical Inner Voice Is Not a Conscience

The critical inner voice is not a conscience or a moral guide. Although the voice may sometimes seem to be related to our values and ideals, its statements against us usually occur after the fact.

The characteristic that most distinguishes the inner voice from a conscience is its degrading, punishing quality. Its demeaning tone tends to increase our feelings of self-hatred instead of motivating us to change undesirable actions in a constructive manner. These destructive thoughts are contradictory; first they influence us to act in self-defeating ways, and then they condemn us for those very actions. In addition, the voice often turns our natural desires, wants, and goals—the things we would like to accomplish in life—into "shoulds"—that is, we "should" do this or that in order to be a good person. When we fail to live up to these "shoulds," the voice ridicules and berates us for our failure.

How Your Critical Inner Voice "Talks" to You

Most people experience their self-attacks in the first person: that is, as "I" statements. Others experience them almost as if someone else were speaking to them. For example, one man referred to his critical inner voices as the "board meeting" in his head.

It is valuable to put these self-attacks into the second person, "you," as though someone else were saying them to you. This practice has three main benefits: (1) it helps you separate the critical point of view of yourself from a more realistic view; (2) it starts to make you think of other negative thoughts that you may not have been aware of before, thoughts that were just below the surface of consciousness; and (3) it brings up feelings that are often associated with these thoughts and makes you aware of the snide or sarcastic tone of your critical inner voice.

Exercise 1.2: Your Critical Inner Voice Attacks

On the left-hand side of the page in exercise 1.2, record your self-attacks as you think them in the first person, "I": for example, "I feel stupid" or "I'm not very good at this kind of work." Next, on the right-hand side of the page, rewrite these statements in the second person, "you": "You're stupid" or "You're not very good at this kind of work."

After you have recorded several thoughts on the right-hand side of the page in the second person, "you," read them aloud. Do you notice whether they have more impact than they did when you wrote them in the first person, "I"? Does this seem to bring anger or other feelings up in you? Do you sound angry when reading them aloud in the second person? Does reading them aloud make you think of other voices you had not thought of before?

Becoming Familiar with Your Critical Inner Voice

The critical inner voice is often experienced as a running commentary in our mind that interprets events and interactions in ways that cause us pain and distress. It is an internal dialogue, a harsh and judgmental way of talking to ourselves. In essence, the voice operates as a filter, making negative interpretations of present-day events based on negative experiences that occurred in the past. The more of these events or losses you experienced in your early life, the more likely you are to interpret present-day situations and interactions in a destructive manner.

In your everyday life, you experience many events and are involved in numerous social interactions, both in your personal relationships and at work. Since your reactions to these events are influenced to a large degree by your inner voice, you may have very different reactions to the same event or interaction depending on your perspective. If you are viewing life through this negative filter, the situation may look bleak and gloomy. However, if you are experiencing your life from the point of view of your real self, the very same situations or events may look bright and optimistic to you.

Therefore, it is important to realize that events that happen to us are often not the primary cause of our distress; instead, trouble usually arises when we interpret these incidents by filtering them through the critical inner voice. When viewing our lives from this perspective, we often feel self-critical or demoralized if we make a mistake, no matter how small or unimportant. Many times, we exaggerate the consequences of our mistakes and tell ourselves that we will continue to fail. We may even tell ourselves that we will never succeed at anything we try and that we should give up altogether.

An increased awareness of this enemy within you can provide you with an understanding of why you are so often compelled to interpret events in a negative way. Recognizing the voice is the first step toward change; you can then begin choosing to ignore the dictates of the voice and living life from a more realistic point of view, free from imagined constraints and limitations.

Exercise 1.3: Keeping a Journal: Your Critical Inner Voice/The Real You

A journal can be an effective tool for helping you identify and challenge your critical inner voice. On the left-hand side of the page in exercise 1.3, record negative thoughts toward yourself that you experience during the day. Be sure to state your critical inner voices in the second person, "you": that is, as though someone were talking *to* you. It is helpful to devote ten to fifteen minutes at the end of your day to recalling the negative thoughts you experienced that day. Just let these thoughts flow. Don't censor yourself. Give full expression to your negative thoughts. Don't be afraid of them. You don't have to believe them or act on them. Getting them out in the open, writing them down, will actually give you more control over them. Get to know all the aspects of your negative thinking. Also, don't worry if the thoughts are not logical. Remember that the voice is irrational and the thoughts often contradict each other. After you have finished writing your critical thoughts on the left-hand side of the page, take some time to go back over them. Check to make sure you have written them all in the second person.

Next, on the right-hand side of the page, in relation to each attack, try to express a more friendly, compassionate, and realistic view of yourself, your qualities, and your reactions. What would a close friend or an objective observer see or say about you and about the situation? Write a more friendly view of yourself on the right-hand side of the page. Make sure to state this compassionate point of view in the first person, with "I" statements. This is not meant to be an exercise where you buoy yourself up with self-affirmative statements, but rather where you look at yourself from an objective but compassionate point of view that comes from the real you. How do *you* really see yourself?

Make several copies of this exercise form and assemble your own journal. Throughout the week, continue to keep a record of the negative thoughts you experience each day, writing them on the left-hand side of the page, with a more compassionate view of yourself on the right-hand side, as described above.

How Your Critical Inner Voice Sees Other People

The voice not only attacks us, it also directs its attacks against other people. Just as we have a split view of ourselves, we also possess diametrically opposed views of significant people in our lives. The fact that we have contradictory views, both toward ourselves and toward others, is another indication of the deep division that exists within all of us. At times, we see our loved ones as lovable and have compassionate, affectionate feelings toward them. At other times, we focus on their faults and think of them in cynical terms. For example, we may find ourselves beginning to think cynically about a mate or friend: *"He's so insensitive, so unfeeling"* or *"She's so childish and irresponsible."* Or about people in general: *"You can't trust anybody. People don't really care. Everyone is looking out for number one, for themselves. You've got to be careful or they'll take advantage of you."*

Negative views of others tend to exist in conjunction with self-depreciating attitudes. People tend to vacillate between blaming themselves for their failures and blaming others. They often alternate between verbalizing their self-attacks and expressing suspicious or prejudicial attitudes toward other people. However, in some people, the tendency to distort others or view them with cynicism and distrust is more prominent than their tendency to attack themselves.

How the Critical Inner Voice Disrupts Your Everyday Life

One of the most powerful strategies for combating the effects of the inner voice is becoming aware of situations and experiences that may lead to your becoming involved in the process of self-attack. You may notice that you sometimes slip into a bad mood or become upset following certain events in your everyday life. The fact that your mood shifts from feeling optimistic or relaxed to feeling down or irritable may be a sign that you are interpreting the event through your internalized voices. Simply recognizing that you are involved in a process of self-attack is valuable in challenging the voice. The next step is to identify the contents of your self-attacking process.

Recognize the Events That Trigger Your Critical Inner Voice

If, during the past week, you observed that your mood switched—for example, from feeling relatively happy and content to feeling down—try to recall the event or interaction that occurred immediately prior to the shift in your feelings. After thinking about the details of the event or conversation, try to remember what you were telling yourself at the time. Although many situations and encounters can be distressing or anxiety-producing, it is important to reemphasize that the way we interpret these events or situations is the crux of the problem. What we tell ourselves about the event, about ourselves, and about the other person or people involved is far more crucial in determining our feelings and our state of mind than the event itself.

For example, Mary and her husband had been married for six years when they decided to separate. Their mutual goal was to eventually divorce, yet they both wanted to maintain their friendship. After several weeks, Mary began to be troubled with some problems related to the terms of the divorce settlement. One day, she noticed that she felt especially terrible, whereas the week before she had felt good and had been optimistic about her future.

Mary sought out a close friend to talk with. Her friend asked her to try to recall any event or interaction that she could identify as having occurred just before her mood changed. Mary immediately remembered a phone conversation she had had with her husband about the financial terms of the divorce settlement:

I just blew up at him because he seemed so unreasonable and arbitrary. He was also critical about my future plans. What difference does it make to him what I do? Anyway, I ended up feeling furious, at him and myself, whereas before the phone call, I really believed things were going well; I thought we were still friends.

As the conversation continued, Mary's friend, who was familiar with the concept of the critical inner voice, asked her what she had been telling herself both during the phone call and afterward. Mary reflected for a moment, then responded:

I think it started before the phone call. I had started having some worries about my financial situation. At the time, they seemed minor, but then when we talked on the phone, I started thinking to myself: *"He sounds like he doesn't have a worry in the world and here you are, all alone, worrying about how you're going to make it. What an inconsiderate jerk! Doesn't he realize what you're going through?"*

Then I said something sort of along those lines to him, and his response made me bristle. Thinking back on it now, I can't even remember what he said, but I started telling myself, *"Look, there he goes again, thinking only about himself. He's so insensitive. Be glad you're rid of him!"*

But after I hung up, I felt much worse. I started attacking myself, thinking, *"Now look at what you've done. You've ruined any chance of having a peaceful settlement."* And I didn't stop there, either. I just kept on ruminating on that theme until I was blaming the breakup of our marriage on myself, like, *"You ruined your marriage by acting this way. Always flying off the handle. You're so stupid. You deserve everything that's happened. It's all your fault."*

The whole evening, I found myself going back and forth between being furious at him and blaming him for everything and pointing the finger of blame at myself. There was no middle ground anywhere in my mind, I just couldn't get a realistic perspective on anything. So I felt discouraged and upset the whole next day and it's kept me from trying to open up the lines of communication with him again. I felt like I was a total failure at simply conveying to him that I was a little worried about my future. I told myself, *"Why even try talking to him? He won't understand anyway."*

Actually, I know that he's probably thinking the same thing. I know for sure that it would be better for me, and for him, to get together and talk about this in a more reasonable way. In fact, while I was telling you my voices, I could see how ridiculous it is for me to continue attacking myself like this. Thinking this way has prevented me from doing what I really wanted to do, which was to express to him in some way my painful feelings about the separation, not to nag him or attack him about some small detail of the financial arrangement. In reality, I have enough money from the settlement to last me a long time.

After Mary identified the angry, cynical thoughts she had toward her husband and revealed her self-attacks to her friend, she looked forward to talking with her husband, and arranged to meet him for dinner that evening. The following day, she was gratified to be able to tell her friend that she had been successful in letting her husband know her real concerns and the painful feelings she was experiencing about their breakup. In talking directly to him about her feelings, she was able to attain her real goal, which was to maintain their friendship in spite of the fact that they would be living separately.

Recognize the Specific Outside Criticisms That Support Your Critical Inner Voice

In trying to identify your specific self-attacks, it is helpful to keep track of your reactions to criticism from friends, family members, coworkers, or employers. It appears that all of us are much more sensitive to feedback when it fits in with specific negative attitudes we already have toward ourselves. In addition, we often overreact to outside criticism, no matter how harsh or mild, realistic or unrealistic, because we imagine it coming from someone as hostile toward us as we are toward ourselves. These reactions of anger, hurt feelings, shame, and guilt are typically out of proportion to the content or severity of the negative feedback people receive.

For example, in an encounter group, an intelligent, attractive woman was confronted by another participant who criticized her angrily, stating that he found her offensive in many ways. His attacks were wide-ranging and quite harsh. The woman sat calmly listening until he called her "stupid," one of the mildest attacks. At that point, she jumped up and yelled, "Don't call me stupid!" Later, after some reflection, she disclosed that when he called her "stupid," she had felt completely devastated and furious. Although on a realistic level she recognized that she was an intelligent woman, when she was a child her family had viewed her as the "stupid" one.

Become Aware of Times You May Be Projecting Your Self-Attacks onto Other People

For some of us, recognizing the division within us is too painful or disconcerting. Consequently, we project our critical inner voices onto other people. In many cases, feeling disapproved of or criticized by another person appears less upsetting than experiencing the painful attacks from within. In general, we find it easier to fight against an outside enemy than to struggle against the enemy within.

It is important to recognize that you may be projecting your own critical inner voices onto other people. At times, you may disown the negative thoughts you are thinking about yourself and instead perceive other people as thinking and feeling those things toward you. In fact, almost every criticism you imagine other people are thinking about you, things that give you a terrible, sinking feeling, are likely to be criticisms that you are thinking about yourself.

For example, a young man who had doubts about his masculinity described this process of projecting his critical inner voice onto women:

> Whenever I meet a woman for the first time, I just know that she is thinking certain things about me. I don't just think or imagine women see me in a negative light. I feel absolutely certain of it. I believe that women, in general, think I'm boyish, not to be taken seriously as a man—a pal, maybe, or someone to joke with, but definitely not a man. It's difficult for me to take back these projections and to see that I'm the one who is thinking this way about myself. Most of the time I act in a way to get that kind of response from women, a response that confirms my belief about what they are thinking.

If this man had remained unaware that his beliefs about what women were thinking of him were projections of his own self-attacks, he would have found it difficult to identify the underlying causes of his self-defeating behavior. In addition, he would have had a tendency to continue to be hesitant in approaching women, thereby insuring rejection. His interactions with women would have continued to confirm his negative image of himself as a man.

Challenging the Critical Inner Voice by Taking Action

Plans for changing actions that are dictated by your critical inner voice fall into two categories: (1) plans for going against negative voices telling you to engage in behaviors that are not in your best interest; and (2) plans for actions that are in your interest—activities or interactions that the inner voice is trying to talk you out of.

As an example of the first type of action, a man drinking with friends after work became aware of a critical inner voice urging him to soothe himself: *"Go ahead, have another drink. You deserve to take the edge off."* Instead of going with what the voice was telling him, he made the decision not to have more than one drink. This action increased his determination to not give in to the dictates of the inner voice in the future and strengthened his own point of view.

An example of the second type of action—doing something in your own interest—involved a woman who was painfully shy. She was afraid to strike up a conversation with a man in her church group whom she felt friendly toward. Every time she approached him, she thought, *"Why would he want to talk to you? You have nothing interesting to say."* In this case, the action she planned was to take a chance and initiate a conversation with him.

When we take these kinds of risks, we enhance our self-esteem and gain strength from being assertive. It requires a certain amount of courage to test negative assumptions like the ones predicting that we are going to be rejected. Real learning and change take place only when we prove to ourselves that our efforts can lead to a different outcome than was predicted by our inner voice.

Taking action to resist self-soothing behaviors also takes integrity and determination: it strengthens our resolve to give up addictive habit patterns that are interfering with our lives. Subsequently, we can take more chances on meeting our needs in more constructive ways. When we continue to take actions in the direction of our wants, desires, and goals even when setbacks occur, we are enhancing our real self and expanding the boundaries of our world.

Exercise 1.4: A Plan for Action

In exercise 1.4, the left-hand side of the page, "Actions dictated by my critical inner voice," is provided for recording the behaviors or habit patterns that you believe are being encouraged or influenced by the voices you have identified. On the right-hand side, "Actions to take that reflect the real me," describe the actions you plan to take that reflect your own point of view rather than the dictates of the voice. These might consist of behaviors that fit in with the interests you are pursuing as well as activities you especially enjoy. These behaviors can consist of small yet increasingly assertive steps that you plan to take in going against the voice. Throughout the week, continue to record the actions that you believe are being controlled by the inner voice as well as the actions you have decided to take on your own behalf.

The most important part of this exercise involves thinking of new behaviors that counter the dictates of your voice. Many people, both in and out of therapy, have been able to make major changes in their lives by doing this. If you recognize a self-defeating pattern of behavior you want to change, you can decide to decrease this behavior, or even drop it altogether. However, it is important to know that by interrupting negative behaviors, you are disrupting your basic defenses. Therefore, it is inevitable that you will experience some level of anxiety while you are in the process of giving up a self-defeating behavior.

Expect Anxiety: It's a Sign of Positive Change

When people begin to change negative views of themselves and behaviors that are based on their critical inner voices, they invariably experience feelings of anxiety. Any change or progress arouses anxiety, and voice attacks usually increase in intensity, but only temporarily. Most people tend to see anxiety as something bad—as indicating something is wrong with them. All of us have been taught to get rid of anxiety: to take a pill or do anything we can to decrease some of the unpleasant sensations associated with it.

Remember that anxiety almost always accompanies emotional growth. It is often an indication that we are making constructive changes in our lives. If we learn to tolerate the increase in anxiety and voice attacks that always accompany any positive change in our ways of thinking about ourselves, the anxiety and voice attacks will gradually decrease or fade into the background. It's as if the voice is attacking us for stepping out of line, for not going along with our internalized negative prescriptions for living. It resembles an angry parent yelling at us, trying to get us back into line. If we sweat it out and stick with the new behavior, the attacks start to recede. The situation is very much like a parent who gets tired of nagging and finally gives up.

Challenging the Critical Inner Voice Through Voice Therapy

The methods of voice therapy were developed to bring destructive thoughts or voices to the surface, together with their accompanying emotions, so that people could challenge them and change the behaviors that are regulated by them. The method is called *voice therapy* because it is a process of giving spoken words to negative thought patterns that govern people's self-limiting, self-destructive behaviors and ways of living.

In therapy sessions, clients learn to express their self-critical thoughts in the second person, "you," in the form of spoken statements *toward* themselves, rather than statements *about* themselves. Saying the voice aloud in this particular format enables clients to separate their own point of view from hostile thoughts and attitudes that make up the alien point of view they acquired early in life. Often, they immediately connect their internalized voices to attitudes and interactions that characterized one or both of their parents. By exposing their negative thoughts and investigating their sources, they disrupt their basic defenses and are able to change their self-concept in a positive direction. People often express many of the feelings associated with the voice and uncover core negative beliefs of which they were previously unaware. In other words, many of their beliefs that existed on an unconscious level emerge during the course of voice therapy.

In a group session, Rick talked about the effect of hearing a mild criticism from his brother. At the time, Rick had been married for ten years, had two children, and was a successful executive in a large company. However, his childhood had been stormier than most; it had been filled with endless arguments between his parents, which created a chaotic atmosphere in the home. He started by describing how his brother's criticism had activated a self-critical thought process. As he began to give words to this attacking voice, he was overcome by powerful emotions. Here is part of this conversation:

Rick: Last week, my brother said that he had some trepidation about my family's coming to stay with him for a while. After the conversation, I was really ripping into myself.

Therapist: What were you telling yourself about what he said?

Rick: The attack as I heard it was that I'm not fit to live with: *"You're just a quiet creep—you're second class. You're just worthless."* I can really feel the attack: *"You're not fit to be around people—and you should really hide it. You should really be careful. You should be quiet and just stay in the background because when people know you, they'll see that you are just a creep!"*

                So then if anyone says anything about my children, I put it in the same attack I felt in my family. I think the basis of the attack is *"You're just like us. What makes you think you're different? You're just a crazy, scummy person."* [Rick began to cry.]

                I really started feeling a lot when I thought about my children, that they get woven into it in that sense, and how strongly I don't want them to have this feeling. I can see that the way I believe this about myself and the way I live my life has given the feeling to them in some way. I know how important it is for me to change this for myself—but also for them, because I felt so bad when I said that just now—when I put words to my feeling that they were creeps because I was a creep.

Later in the session, Rick discovered that his feelings of futility about making constructive changes in his life had their origins in the pessimistic views his own father had about life:

Rick: The voice said: *"Even if you feel a lot today, what are you going to do, because there's still nothing there. You're still nothing."* It says there's nothing there, that I have no substance.

Therapist: How did you get a feeling like that?

Rick: I didn't see my father as having any power. Like, he always dreamed of having a boat, and he would go to look at boats in the marina on the weekends. But he never did anything about it. I didn't see him doing anything or taking any action. It was all a fantasy.

Several weeks later, Rick talked about the improvements he noticed in himself and in his relationship with his children following the session:

I could particularly see my son feeling better because I was relating to him in a different way. I became much more happy to see him, like really a joyful feeling to come home from work and see him. And my daughter to a degree, but for some reason, my son—I think I see myself in my son. So just to see him as a separate person and to feel what I want for him, what I would have wanted for myself in terms of what I didn't have growing up, still causes me some pain and sadness. But I feel great trying to give that to him.

In voice therapy, the process of identifying the voice attacks and expressing the accompanying emotions allows the patient to regain his or her own perspective and feeling for himself or herself. In essence, the patient has reconnected to himself or herself. Certain forms of therapy recommend making statements of self-affirmation as a way of answering back to this negative point of view. But paradoxically, patting yourself on the back can later lead to a childish reaction, such as an increase in self-defeating behavior. Praising ourselves in this manner is as damaging as punishing ourselves because it is as though we were standing outside ourselves. In both cases, we are one step removed from ourselves and our experiences and are therefore not really living our lives. It is of the utmost importance to be ourselves and to experience our emotions directly rather than observing or attending to ourselves.

The next step in voice therapy, changing the behaviors that are based on the critical inner voice, is a powerful and important answer to our critical inner voices. We are in essence saying back to the inner voice: "I don't have to do what you say. I am going to live the life I want and pursue my own goals and desires."

To summarize, a destructive thought process of sabotage and self-attack exists within all of us. We are plagued to varying degrees by an internal dialogue that is harmful, restrictive, and ultimately self-destructive. Voice therapy methods give spoken words to the inner enemy and to its ways of viewing us and our life. Journaling, setting goals for changing the behaviors controlled by the voice, and taking action in a step-by-step manner can be invaluable in counteracting the dictates of the voice.

By becoming aware of our critical inner voice and going against its dictates, we are beginning to address the questions: Are we are living out our own lives and fulfilling our own destinies, or are we repeating patterns of the past and reliving our parents' lives? Are we being ruled by the way our critical inner voice views us or by attitudes that express our real self? The more we are able to break with our negative parental prescriptions for living, the greater the opportunity we have for fulfilling our own destiny.

Exercise 1.1: Visualizing the Real You

My physical abilities:

_____

_____

_____

My positive qualities:

_____

_____

_____

My interests and activities:

_____

_____

_____

My long-term goals:

_____

_____

_____

My short-term goals:

_____

_____

_____

Where do I stand in relation to my goals?

_____

_____

_____

Exercise 1.2: Your Critical Inner Voice Attacks

Self-critical attacks as "I" statements	**Self-critical attacks** as "you" statements
Example: "I don't think I'm an attractive person."	Example: "You're not attractive."

Exercise 1.3: Keeping a Journal:
Your Critical Inner Voice/The Real You

My critical inner voice as "you" statements Example: "You're so stupid."	**The real me** as "I" statements Example: "Sometimes I struggle with work, but I catch on quickly and then usually do a good job."

Exercise 1.4: A Plan for Action

Actions dictated by my critical inner voice	Actions to take that reflect the real me

Chapter 2

How Your Critical Inner Voice Creates Shame, Guilt, and Low Self-Esteem

It is only too easy to compel a sensitive human being to feel guilty about anything.

—Morton Irving Seiden

Shame and guilt are the primary emotions that contribute to low self-esteem. In fact, most of us spend our lives within a restrictive range of personal relationships and experiences that are bound by feelings of guilt and shame.

A distinction can be made between shame and guilt. *Shame* is the emotion we feel when we see ourselves as inherently inferior or deficient in some way. *Guilt* is related to our behavior; for example, when we think we have done something wrong or when we fail to live up to our own ideals and values. Often these emotions are stimulated by our critical inner voice. Frequently, these unrealistic, negative emotions lower our self-esteem, make us feel we are not worthwhile people, and diminish our feelings of positive self-regard. In learning how to overcome feelings of shame and guilt, we need to identify these emotions when they occur and then uncover the critical inner voices that influence and intensify them.

Identify When You Are Feeling Shame or Guilt

Shame is a primitive feeling that develops early in childhood, perhaps even before children learn to talk. It is a deep-seated sense that we were born bad and unlovable. It is a depressing feeling because it feels like it is something we are helpless to change or affect in any way. Many of us grow up feeling ashamed of our desire for affection—for wanting to be touched, loved, and really seen and understood by other people. When we feel ashamed or humiliated, we often want to cover up any signs we perceive in ourselves that might indicate to other people that we are basically bad.

If our parents had negative views about nudity and the human body, we, as children, tended to take on these views as our own and developed a sense of shame about our bodies and our sexual feelings. Research studies have shown, for example, that severe, harsh, or intrusive toilet training arouses feelings of shame in children and is connected to later emotional and sexual disturbances. These negative feelings that we develop about our bodies and our sexuality are often retained throughout life and can cause serious problems in our intimate relationships.

Guilt can be defined as self-critical feelings and attitudes that are experienced in relation to our actions, as well as in relation to thoughts and feelings that we see as unacceptable. Guilt is aroused when we recognize that we have done something wrong or hurt another person's feelings. We may also feel guilty if we secretly wish for something bad to happen to someone we dislike. And although we feel happy when we win out over a rival in a competitive situation, or when we achieve more success than a friend or family member, on another level we may feel guilty. However, even in situations where you know you are in the wrong, it serves no purpose to attack yourself for the negative effects of your behavior. It is much more constructive to identify the critical inner voices that intensify your guilty feelings, feel compassion for yourself and the other person, and plan ways to change your behavior in future interactions.

There are two distinct forms of guilt that create a basic conflict in people: guilt about moving toward our goals and pursuing our wants (*neurotic guilt*) and guilt about giving up and retreating from really living our lives (*existential guilt*). The first kind of guilt is experienced as feelings of remorse or self-accusation for seeking satisfaction in life. Essentially, we accuse ourselves of being "selfish" when we are simply pursuing our own personal and career goals.

If, however, we submit to this guilt and retreat from pursuing our goals, we experience the second kind of guilt. This type of guilt is awakened when we hold back our natural tendencies to fulfill ourselves in life, become passive, or seek satisfaction in fantasy. This painful emotion, which is a combination of grief and remorse, can be a signal that, for whatever reason, you have wandered from the path that reflects your own wants, ideals, and values.

All of us are in an emotional catch-22—that is, we are suspended between these two poles of guilt, and they determine the limits of our life experience. If we move toward realizing our personal goals in life, we feel neurotic guilt, yet if we give up and do not try, we feel existential guilt.

The Defenses on Which Guilt, Shame, and Low Self-Esteem Are Based

It appears that many of us grew up thinking of ourselves as bad or unlovable, and as adults, we tend to feel ashamed and guilty in many situations. But why can't we allow new relationships with people who genuinely admire and love us to modify how we see ourselves in a positive direction? Why don't we simply adopt a more realistic view of ourselves after we discover that we have been seriously distorting ourselves? The answer lies in the fact that these negative beliefs are a fundamental part of a system of defenses we needed to build when we were small, weak, and vulnerable. As described in chapter 1, these defensive methods protected us against emotional pain and actually helped us survive emotionally at a critical time in life.

Picture defenses like the protective armor that knights used in medieval times to survive in battle. Now imagine the situation of wearing the heavy armor when there is no longer any danger. The armor of your defenses protected you when you were young, but if you continue to wear it as an adult, your ability to move freely will be seriously restricted. Yet how do you know when it is safe to take it off? As you give up your defenses, you must first take the risk of throwing off your armor, even before you find out that you are safe. This situation is anxiety-provoking, and many people prefer to remain "safe" within their armor.

The defense of continuing to believe the critical inner voice—the lack of trust, the cynicism, the things you keep secret because you're ashamed or feel guilty—hurts you far more than any external event in your life today. As a child, you did not have the power to take active measures to cope with stress and pain. You defended yourself as best you could under the circumstances. However, the same defenses that worked when you were a child have persisted beyond childhood and have become self-defeating as you apply them to people and events in your present-day life.

Why We Need to See Our Parents as All Good and All-Powerful

One of the major ways many of us learned to protect ourselves while growing up was to idealize our parents and see ourselves as bad. Idealizing our parents and family is a basic defense, and it's a major source of low self-esteem and of a negative self-image. Young children need to believe that their parents are good and strong, or at least adequate, because a young child's survival literally depends on his or her parents. Therefore, if a child is rejected or unloved by his or her parents, it is more optimistic for the child to attribute the rejection to his or her innate badness than to see the parents as inadequate or unloving. This way, there is always the hope, which children cling to with their whole being, that if they work hard to change themselves and become "good," some day their parents will love them.

Idealizing our parents and family is a fundamental part of our strong resistance to changing our self-image in a positive direction and being able to accept love in our lives. The taboo against exposing parents' inadequacies, weaknesses, or negative traits and behaviors is strong in our society. How many times have you heard relatives and friends tell a child, "Your father really loves you. He just doesn't know how to show it," when in fact he has been insensitive to or disrespectful of the child? In the name of protecting children, people are reluctant to criticize a child's parents in the youngster's presence. However, this supports both children's denial of their parents' flaws and shortcomings and their own feeling that they (the children) are at fault.

Exercise 2.1: Seeing Your Parents Realistically

To strengthen your feelings of positive self-regard, it is important to develop a more realistic view of your parents. Remember that your parents were once children who, like you, probably suffered from their own parents' limitations and inadequacies. The goal is not to blame our parents, but rather to attempt to account for our limitations by exploring the events in our early lives that still have negative effects in the present. In addition, as adults we now have the power to take control over our lives, which we did not have as children. When we develop a more realistic picture of our parents and clearly see their weaknesses as well as their strengths, we are taking an important step toward changing our self-image in a positive direction.

In exercise 2.1 (at the end of the chapter), record your answers to the questions in part A ("Describing Your Parents' Traits and Behaviors") and part B ("Your Parents' Behaviors That May Have Caused You Shame or Guilt"). The first four questions in part A are taken from the parents' workbooks used in the compassionate child-rearing parent education program (described in Firestone's *Compassionate Child-Rearing* [1990]). When mothers and fathers explore important events in their childhoods and the child-rearing practices used by their parents, and describe their parents' positive and negative traits, they develop more compassion for themselves and increase their feelings of positive self-regard. Developing a more realistic view of their parents allows them to see themselves from a more realistic, positive perspective.

The questions in part B are taken from the English version of the Swedish EMBU (Swedish acronym for *Egna Minnen Betrdffande Uppfostram*, "My Memories of Upbringing") inventory (Perris, Jaconsson, Lindström, van Knorring, and Perris 1980), which measures, among other parental behaviors, those that generate shame and guilt in children. These questions may be answered with a yes or a no.

Critical Inner Voices Underlying Neurotic Guilt

Many of us experience neurotic guilt in the form of critical inner voices. When we suffer excessive frustration or are emotionally deprived early in life, we tend to develop a negative self-image. As adults, we often turn away from pleasurable experiences and limit our lives because on some level we are telling ourselves that we don't deserve to be happy or successful.

How Your Critical Inner Voice Makes You Feel Guilty about Pursuing Your Wants

Guilt reactions arise early in life as a result of parents' rejecting attitudes in relation to their children's pursuit of simple needs—both their need for practical care and their need for affectionate contact and love. When children's wants and needs are frustrated, they invariably blame themselves for being needy, and develop feelings of guilt.

For example, Chris, twenty-three, was single and hard-working, and earned a good living as a tax accountant. However, since he was a teenager he had been interested in working more directly with people in a helping profession or in public service. He enrolled in night school, taking courses in psychology and sociology, and found the classes to be the most exciting part of his life. He decided to work only part-time and use his savings to go back to school. He hoped to eventually obtain a graduate degree in psychology. Upon giving notice at work, he was besieged by strong voice attacks, telling him he was making a terrible mistake:

> *"You're really burning your bridges behind you, aren't you? Who do you think you are, anyway, changing your career at this point in your life? Giving up a great job, and for what? What makes you think you're smart enough to get through graduate school? You're never going to make it through. You'll just change your mind again. You were always like this, so irresponsible! You should just be content with the job you have. Why can't you be like us? Why can't you just settle down?"*

After identifying his self-attacks, Chris was relieved, and felt much stronger about his decision. He also had an important insight about the origins of these critical inner voices. He remembered his father complaining about being stuck in a boring job, but never doing anything about it. In addition, both of Chris's parents led rigid, restricted lives, and they had put considerable pressure on him to find a steady, secure job immediately after he finished business school. Chris recognized that he felt guilty about the possibility of surpassing his father by having a job that he was excited about.

How Your Critical Inner Voice Makes You Feel Guilty About Being Alive

As noted in chapter 1, the critical inner voice is a negative point of view assimilated from parents at times when they were angry, punishing, or rejecting. If, for example, you were unwanted or were born at a difficult time for your parents, you may have grown up believing that you were a burden. If so, it is likely that, as an adult, you would feel that you are unworthy of love. On an even deeper level, you may feel guilty for even being alive.

For example, Cynthia, who was the third of three children and the product of an unplanned pregnancy, expressed guilty thoughts that were triggered when she received news of her older brother's death:

I always felt like I wasn't supposed to have been born. [She began to cry.] I mean, I kind of sneaked in—that's what I feel like. In my whole life, I feel like I just kind of sneaked in. And now that my brother is dead, I feel it even more strongly. It's hard for me to be happy with everything I have in my life today. I have thoughts like, *"What right do you have to be happy? He's dead and he was the good one. Everybody liked him. You're the one who was always a troublemaker. Why should you be happy?"* I was never supposed to have a life, much less a life like I have now.

I wasn't even supposed to be born. It's like nobody was happy that I was born. So in a way, I don't even believe people who say they like me. I'm very skeptical. I don't believe on some basic level that I could be somebody that anyone would like or care about.

Three years prior to this interview, Cynthia's eleven-year-old daughter, Bianca, had revealed similar voices in a children's discussion group. Although Bianca's birth was planned and she was really wanted by her parents, she had somehow taken on the same critical inner voices as her mother had, that she was unworthy and undeserving:

I have voices a lot of the time. They're like, *"You should stop bothering everybody and making trouble. No one cares about you.* [She began to cry.] *No one wants to give anything to you. No one wants to be nice to you, because you're not nice to them. Everybody hates you! You shouldn't have been born in the first place."*

When the group leader asked where she thought that idea came from, Bianca said:

I don't know. Sometimes when I look at my mom or dad, I think that they think of me like that. And that if they didn't think of me like that, they'd be nicer. They wouldn't be so cold.

How Your Critical Inner Voice Makes You Feel Guilty About Standing Out from Your Family

Many people experience painful guilt reactions and voice attacks when they accomplish more in life than a parent did. More often, but not always, it is the parent of the same sex that we feel guilty in relation to. If you achieve more financial or career success, develop more friendships, or have a more satisfying relationship than members of your family, this can arouse a good deal of anxiety and lead to feelings of remorse and self-reproach. People often suffer feelings of guilt about succeeding where family members have failed. Your achievements may trigger negative thoughts or strong voice attacks, such as: *"Who do you think you are? Do you think you're better than us? You only think of yourself."*

For example, David, thirty-five, recently assumed a leadership position at his company. The characteristics that earned him the promotion were his assertiveness and decisiveness, as well as his sensitivity to employees, which was based on his sense of fairness and equality. In contrast, David's father, who tended to be authoritarian and somewhat vain, had failed repeatedly in his business ventures. David realized that the feelings of guilt he was experiencing arose when he obtained a position higher than his father had achieved in business. He began to have doubts about his ability to perform at the executive level. In a journal, he identified the voice attacks he was having.

Here is an excerpt from David's journal (based on exercise 1.3 in chapter 1):

My critical inner voice	The real me
Just shut up and take your place.	I feel good in this position. I belong here. I am valued for what I do and for what I offer.
Don't try to be better than you are.	I'm not trying to be anything. I'm being who I am, and I am where I deserve to be.
Your employees aren't going to be able to stand you.	I care about my employees. I treat them with respect and fairness. They not only like me as a person, but as a manager, too.
You're a tyrant!	I'm not a tyrant. My father was, but I am very different with people than he was.

After clarifying these angry voices and then stating how he really saw himself, David was successful in his struggle against his urges to retreat from the position of authority and sabotage his success. He could see that the self-attacks labeling him a tyrant were blatantly wrong; these voices actually described his father's personality and behavior rather than his own.

Neurotic guilt is also complicated by our fear of losing the fantasy bond or imaginary connection with important people in our lives, including our parents. When we begin to have a more independent life, we feel guilty about separating from these fantasized connections.

Critical Inner Voices Underlying Existential Guilt

Whenever we give in to the critical inner voice of neurotic guilt, we tend to engage in behaviors that are self-defeating and self-limiting. We may sabotage a hard-earned success or turn away from an especially satisfying relationship. However, later we experience feelings of remorse and angry self-attacks for acting in ways that go against our goals and priorities.

How Your Critical Inner Voice Makes You Feel Guilty About Turning Your Back on Your Goals

When people retreat from pursuing life fully, they feel guilty of betraying themselves and, incidentally, of betraying their loved ones. In general, whenever people hold back their talents and positive traits or pull back from being close to and affectionate with a relationship partner, they cannot help but feel guilty.

For example, in the months following the birth of her first child, Sara became gloomy and somewhat depressed. She appeared to be overwhelmed by the responsibilities of motherhood, and she felt inadequate. She was tense and distracted and became remote and distant from her husband, Jack. At times when her baby cried during the night she had a hard time stifling her feelings of resentment. Sara wanted to get a grip on the negative thoughts that were causing her to go against something she had wanted so badly. She began to write her thoughts in a journal:

My critical inner voice	The real me
You don't know how to take care of a baby.	It's true I'm a new mother, but I do have some good instincts about taking care of my baby. And what I don't know, I can learn.
You just make him feel bad.	He does cry and feel bad sometimes, but all babies cry. If I'm calm and relaxed, I can usually make him feel better.
You're not the kind of woman who should have children.	I love Jack and we want to have a family together. We want to offer our children a good life. So I am the kind of woman who should have children.

You're such a bad mother.	There's no such thing as a perfect mother. Just like in any other relationship, you learn about yourself and grow. I'm not a bad mother. I'm a mother.
Don't you see you're making Jack feel bad, too?	Realistically, I haven't been myself lately, and he misses me. I miss being close to him, too.
He's going to lose interest in you.	He's not going to reject me just because I'm going through a hard time. His love is deeper than that.
He doesn't think you can handle a baby either, and he's right.	The way he looks at it, we're both new at this. We're both learning how to be parents. We're in this together.
You should never have gotten yourself into this.	That's ridiculous. These two relationships are the joys of my life. I expect some bumps along the way, but they won't stop me!

After writing in her journal, it became clear to Sara that her self-attacks had led to her being distant from her husband and baby. This distance brought up tremendous feelings of guilt which made her feel even more distant from her family. Over the next few weeks, Sara continued to identify her voice attacks and learned how to deal with many of the unfamiliar emotions that had been triggered by the birth of her baby. She became more optimistic and gradually modified the unrealistic, self-depreciating thoughts that told her she was inadequate in caring for her baby. She was then able to once again enjoy a close relationship with her husband.

When we live our own lives instead of automatically living out the life that was prescribed for us, we will tend to experience neurotic guilt. However, if we become overwhelmed by this type of guilt and start giving up living by our own standards and values, or if we withdraw from a valued relationship, we will tend to experience existential guilt. Understanding where these feelings come from, and identifying the voices that trigger them and intensify them, will enable you to interrupt this process of self-attack and regain a sense of compassion for yourself and your unique point of view.

Combating Guilt, Shame, and Low Self-Esteem

There are a number of exercises you can use to challenge and overcome critical inner voices that make you feel ashamed or guilty. As you identify and counter these destructive thoughts, you can feel freer to pursue your life.

Make a Distinction Between the Critical Inner Voice and a Conscience

In identifying self-attacks associated with guilt, it is important to remember that the voice is not a conscience or a moral guide. The voice is irrational, illogical, and contradictory: first it influences us to act in self-defeating ways, and then it condemns us for those very actions. In effect, the voice puts us in a no-win situation. In addition, if the voice were a true conscience, it would not have a tone of sarcasm or ridicule, nor would it possess a harsh, punishing quality. The "shoulds" and "ought tos" that we experience from the voice exert a heavy pressure on us, undermining our energy and motivation rather than inspiring us to try to change actions we recognize as being self-defeating or self-destructive.

Identify Voices That Cause or Intensify Guilt and Shame

Becoming familiar with what you are telling yourself when you feel guilty or humiliated is a first step in challenging these debilitating emotions. After identifying your destructive thoughts, you can learn to separate these negative beliefs from a more realistic point of view, as described in chapter 1. First, try to recall situations that have made you feel guilty or ashamed recently. Which voices did you experience when you were in the situation, or afterward?

Exercise 2.2: The Firestone Voice Scale for Shame and Guilt

Use this exercise to identify how often you experience negative thoughts that make you feel guilty or ashamed.

Exercise 2.3: Shame and Guilt: Your Critical Inner Voices/The Real You

On the left-hand side of the page, record the negative thoughts or beliefs for which you circled a 2, 3, or 4 in exercise 2.2. The voice statements on the list may have reminded you of other thoughts you have experienced that are not included in the list. If so, record those thoughts, too. Then, on the right-hand side, describe a more congenial and realistic view of yourself and your actions. For example, if you scored 2 or more on the item, *"You never do or give enough,"* you might feel like writing several statements on your own behalf, such as, "Actually, I'm a pretty generous person. I feel like doing things for other people a lot of the time. Sometimes when I'm preoccupied with a problem, I may not be as generous or giving as I usually am, but those times are an exception." Take time to really think about and formulate answers to the guilt- and shame-provoking voices you experience.

A few of the negative voices or beliefs may have some basis in reality, such as, *"You're too shy and reserved."* However, even if a person is shy, the self-attack about being shy and reserved is harsh and judgmental and is typically followed by a moralistic "should" statement. Categorical statements about oneself that are followed by prescriptions and "shoulds" are not conducive to making changes.

Identify Seemingly Positive Thoughts That Disguise Low Self-Esteem

In many of the trainings we conduct for therapists, the participants ask: "What about positive voices? Don't people have any positive voices?" The critical inner voice, by definition, is a destructive process by which the person is detached from the self, and relates to himself or herself as an object. People do have voices that are seemingly positive, but these voices often have a destructive effect on a person's behavior, feelings, and life. For example, there are the apparently friendly voices that encourage people to back away from their goals, such as: *"You deserve a break. You can finish that project later."* These voices are destructive in that they set the person up to feel guilty later on for procrastinating and not accomplishing his or her goal.

Many people use positive "self-talk" in an effort to convince themselves that they are okay or to reassure themselves that they have no self-doubts or bad feelings about themselves. For example, Larry, a man with presumably high self-esteem, recently consulted an industrial psychologist because he wanted to improve his managerial skills.

In the initial interview, which explored his personal history in all areas, Larry said he had no problems in making friends or in his personal relationships, although he was divorced. The only thing that troubled him, he said, was his habit of being indecisive in his new position as systems manager for a large company.

When the psychologist asked Larry how he saw himself in general, and how he felt about himself, he replied that he had a really good opinion of himself, felt very self-assured and self-confident. He declared, with some pride, that he was a "self-made" man and had worked hard to get to the position he presently held. He said that he admired himself for this achievement. The only blemish on this otherwise perfect picture of high self-esteem was that Larry tended to second-guess himself about decisions he had to make in his new job. This made him feel anxious and at times almost paralyzed in stressful situations that demanded a quick response on his part.

The psychologist encouraged Larry to explore the feelings he had when he was indecisive. Larry began to recognize that his self-confidence and high self-esteem were only a thin veneer covering a deep sense of being weak, ineffective, and basically defective. When Larry became aware of his critical inner voice behind his feelings of inferiority and shame, as well as the rage that emerged as he exposed these feelings, he steadily progressed and became more straightforward and resolute in making decisions. Part of his therapy consisted of uncovering and identifying specific voice attacks that told him he was incompetent and second class. He remarked that until he became aware of these negative voices—his "dark side," as he called it—he had not felt entirely "real" in his interactions at work or in his relationships.

From this example, you can see that some people are not always aware of the negative thoughts and beliefs they have. In fact, if asked, these people probably would say that they really like or approve of themselves a good deal of the time. On an intellectual level, they may be telling the truth, as far as they know the truth. Still, their actions and the way they conduct their lives often show that, on an emotional level, they are harboring self-depreciating attitudes and considerable anger toward themselves.

The "Positive" Voice of Vanity: A Cover-up for Low Self-Esteem

The thoughts that underlie vanity are tricky and deceptive simply because they are seemingly positive, approving, and protective. In identifying and challenging the critical inner voice, it is valuable to become aware of the "positive" voice of vanity. Many of us have destructive thoughts that at first glance appear to be in our best interests, as did the thoughts that Larry experienced. Among these ostensibly friendly voices are thoughts of exaggerated self-importance and competence that we use to compensate for feelings of inferiority we developed early in life. These internalized voices camouflage a negative self-image and feelings of low self-esteem.

Many people have an internal dialogue that builds them up to help conceal the fact that they are tearing themselves down. This is the voice of vanity—the flip side of the coin of low self-esteem. These "positive" voices are the ones that falsely reassure people that they have exceptional talents or an ability to perform at unrealistically high levels. Often, these stem from a parent building up the child as a substitute for loving the child; or needing the child to be great as a reflection on him or her. Later, after these individuals have failed to live up to their self-imposed standards, the voice can be merciless in its condemnation. In other words, this type of voice is a set-up for failure and for subsequent feelings of demoralization and humiliation.

As a child, Anne was built up by her mother in relation to her budding talents in art. Anne's mother told her that someday she would be a great artist. In addition, she continually bragged to friends and neighbors about her daughter's abilities.

As an adult, Anne became an art instructor, and painted only occasionally as a hobby. However, deep in her heart, she continued to believe her mother's predictions about her future. One day, Anne saw a poster announcing a competitive art exhibit and decided to enter several of her paintings. She worked hard preparing for the competition, telling herself, *"You're really talented! You can win, if you really set your mind to it. You're just a natural artist."* When her work failed to receive even an honorable mention in the competition, she was deeply humiliated in front of her friends and students. She became despondent and even considered giving up painting altogether.

Finally, Anne sought professional help and began to uncover the thoughts that were contributing to her dejected mood: *"You're not a real artist. You're an imposter! Your work looked pathetic compared to the other entries. You're such a joke! And you actually thought you were in the big leagues, that you were a great artist. How stupid!"*

Next, Anne explored the "positive" thoughts that had set her up for these harsh condemnations. She recognized that this vain point of view was not really her own, but reflected her mother's exaggerated appraisals of her ability, and an attempt to live off her daughter's accomplishments. This insight gave her immediate relief. Anne also had to face the painful truth that her mother's build-up was merely a substitute for the love and affection she had been unable to offer her daughter.

In a later session, she recalled that her mother had told her friends that her daughter's talent was inherited from her. Recognizing that her talents had been exploited by her mother generated new energy in Anne. She also had a more realistic view of herself. She knew that with concerted effort and study she might someday become an artist, but that she would probably never be "great," as her mother had claimed she would. She enrolled in an advanced painting class to obtain further experience with oil painting, which she truly enjoyed, and continued to get considerable pleasure from her teaching.

In general, people find it easier to accept flattery or false praise than genuine admiration and love, because a build-up does not threaten their negative beliefs about themselves. It is not uncommon for people to dismiss a genuine compliment from someone who really admires them and appreciates their personal qualities. They feel awkward and uncomfortable because this experience causes anxiety, self-consciousness, and guilt about standing out.

Exercise 2.4: The Firestone Voice Scale for Vanity

Use exercise 2.4 at the end of the chapter to help you identify these seemingly positive voices of vanity. Check the frequency with which you have experienced the thoughts listed on the scale.

As you were filling out the scale in exercise 2.4, could you recall your parents describing you in these terms? Were their statements accurate descriptions of you, or do you think they were more like a build-up of some real talents or characteristics you possess? Did their praise seem excessive? Do their descriptions of you seem to reflect more of what they wanted to accomplish in their own lives? Did their praise appear to indicate a need on their part for you to be "great" in a way that would enhance their own self-esteem?

Exercise 2.5: How Your Parents Saw You
How You See Yourself

Review the abilities and qualities that you listed in exercise 1.1, Visualizing the Real You (in chapter 1). In exercise 2.5, on the left-hand side of the page, first describe how your parents saw your positive traits. How did they describe your abilities, positive qualities, talents, and special interests? Next, in the right-hand column, describe a realistic evaluation of your positive qualities, physical abilities, talents, and special interests. How do you really see yourself? Are there discrepancies between these two views? Do you ever feel like a failure when you don't live up to your parents' descriptions of you?

Exercise 2.6: Realistic or Imaginary Limitations?

This exercise can help you rethink your limitations—to seriously consider whether or not they are entirely realistic. Perhaps some of these "liabilities" have been controlled by your inner voice: either the voice of vanity that tries to cover over these limitations, or negative thoughts that exaggerate them. Both kinds of thoughts, overly positive or overly negative, can be identified and challenged. Using exercise 2.6, write down what you consider are realistic limitations that may be preventing you from attaining your short-term or long-term goals, as well as those you think are influenced by your critical inner voice.

It is just as important to develop a realistic, balanced view of yourself as it is to develop a realistic view of your parents. To counter feelings of low self-esteem, you need to develop an accepting and understanding attitude in relation to your limitations as you move toward fulfilling your short-term and long-term goals in life. Even though these limitations may present real obstacles as you strive to attain these goals, you need to fight against the tendency that we all have to attack ourselves for our limitations, whether they are imagined or real.

All of us have a basic conflict between fulfilling ourselves in life and sabotaging or limiting ourselves, and we are often unaware of the circle of shame and guilt that keeps us imprisoned in this conflict and that binds us to the past. The techniques and exercises described in this chapter, which are derived from voice therapy techniques, can help you isolate and become conscious of your feelings of shame and guilt. Gaining insight into how these negative thoughts are related to your early life can lead to a deeper understanding of the critical inner voices underlying these painful emotions. By consistently challenging your self-attacks, you can become freer to pursue your life with enthusiasm and vitality.

Exercise 2.1: Seeing Your Parents Realistically
A. Describing Your Parents' Traits and Behaviors

1. Did you experience any long-term separations from your parent or parents during your childhood? Through death? Divorce? Illness? If so, describe your reactions at the time.

_____

_____

_____

_____

2. What do you think your parents offered you that has been the most valuable to you in your adult life? Describe these traits, values, or ideals.

_____

_____

_____

_____

3. What faults or weaknesses did you dislike in your parent or parents? Describe these traits.

_____

_____

_____

_____

4. Were your parents strict or overly permissive in their discipline of you and your siblings? Describe an example of how they disciplined you.

_____

_____

_____

_____

B. Your Parents' Behaviors That May Have Caused You Shame or Guilt

Mother		Father		
Yes	No	Yes	No	1. As a child, were you beaten or scolded in the presence of others?
Yes	No	Yes	No	2. Did your parents show with words and gestures that they liked you?
Yes	No	Yes	No	3. Did it happen that your parents talked about something you had said or done in front of others, so that you felt ashamed?
Yes	No	Yes	No	4. Did your parents begrudge you things you needed?
Yes	No	Yes	No	5. Did your parents criticize you and tell you how lazy and useless you were in front of others?
Yes	No	Yes	No	6. Did your parents use expressions like, "If you do that, you will make me sad?"
Yes	No	Yes	No	7. Did you feel your parents thought it was your fault when they were unhappy?
Yes	No	Yes	No	8. Did your parents use expressions like, "Is this the thanks we get for having done so much for you, and for having sacrificed so much for your sake"?
Yes	No	Yes	No	9. Did it happen that you got a bad conscience toward your parents because you behaved in a way they did not desire?
Yes	No	Yes	No	10. Did your parents say things like, "You who are so big (or you who are a boy/girl) shouldn't act like that, should you"?
Yes	No	Yes	No	11. Did your parents express the wish that you had been like somebody else?
Yes	No	Yes	No	12. Do you think that either of your parents wished you had been different in any way?
Yes	No	Yes	No	13. Would your parents look sad or in any other way show that you had behaved badly, so that you got real feelings of guilt?

Exercise 2.2: The Firestone Voice Scale for Shame and Guilt

Circle the frequency with which you experience the following critical inner voices:

0 = Never   1 = Rarely   2 = Once in a While   3 = Frequently   4 = Most of the Time

Example, you think or say to yourself:

0 1 2③4   You're so stupid.

---

0 1 2 3 4   When people get to know you better, they'll see how terrible you really are.

0 1 2 3 4   You had another car accident? You're such a klutz!

0 1 2 3 4   Look at all the problems you cause.

0 1 2 3 4   No one wants to hear what you have to say. You should just keep your opinions to yourself.

0 1 2 3 4   You're so unlovable. How could he (she) care about you?

0 1 2 3 4   You forgot to pay that bill. Can't you do anything right?

0 1 2 3 4   You don't deserve anything.

0 1 2 3 4   You're so awkward and self-conscious. No wonder you don't have any friends.

0 1 2 3 4   You wanted a baby so much and now you're not spending any time with him (her).

0 1 2 3 4   You dressed all wrong for this dinner. Everybody's staring at you.

0 1 2 3 4   Just look at yourself! You're so unattractive. You're so ugly.

0 1 2 3 4   You're a failure at everything you try.

0 1 2 3 4   You wanted to be successful and now look at you! You've given up all your goals and you're just drifting along.

0 1 2 3 4   You're such miserable company to be with.

0 1 2 3 4   You just don't belong here. You're different from everyone else.

0 1 2 3 4   What happened to all those dreams you had when you were young? You haven't accomplished anything you set out to do.

0 1 2 3 4   You don't deserve happiness. You're such a creep.

0 1 2 3 4   You're too shy and reserved. You should be more assertive.

0 1 2 3 4   Why can't you be more like your brother (sister)?

0 1 2 3 4   The things you believe about yourself are real. You really are useless.

0 1 2 3 4   You really hurt him (her). How will you ever ask for forgiveness?

0 1 2 3 4   What makes you so special?

0 1 2 3 4   You never do or give enough.

0 1 2 3 4   Who do you think you are, anyway? You're no different from us [family].

0 1 2 3 4   So you thought you could go off and make a life for yourself. Well, you can't. You can't have anything.

0 1 2 3 4   You're so inconsiderate. All you think about is yourself. You never think about your family (children, mother, father).

Exercise 2.3: Shame and Guilt:
Your Critical Inner Voice/The Real You

My critical inner voices that cause shame and guilt	My realistic view of myself

Exercise 2.4: The Firestone Voice Scale for Vanity

Circle the frequency with which you experience the following "positive" self-statements:

0 = Never 1 = Rarely 2 = Once in a while 3 = Frequently 4 = Most of the Time

0 1 2 3 4   You're much smarter and have a lot more going for you than your friends.

0 1 2 3 4   You can accomplish anything! Nothing is too hard for you.

0 1 2 3 4   You have so much talent! Someday people will appreciate what you have to offer.

0 1 2 3 4   You know how to cope better than other people. Nothing ever gets you down.

0 1 2 3 4   Most people are really screwed up, but you always have things under control.

0 1 2 3 4   Sure she's beautiful, but beauty is only skin deep. You've got more personality and charm.

0 1 2 3 4   He doesn't know how to treat women sensitively like you do.

0 1 2 3 4   You give everything to this relationship, and he (she) gives almost nothing.

0 1 2 3 4   You deserve a promotion. Nobody contributes to this company more than you do.

0 1 2 3 4   The things you do are so valuable. You're indispensable. How could people at work get along without you?

0 1 2 3 4   You should get credit for that project. You did most of the work.

0 1 2 3 4   You're the real brains behind this operation.

0 1 2 3 4   You've got everything going for you: good looks, personality, charm. You're really going to go places.

0 1 2 3 4   Of course women prefer you over other men.

0 1 2 3 4   You have such a great sense of humor. Look how he's (she's) laughing at your jokes.

0 1 2 3 4   Just look around. It's obvious you're the prettiest woman (best looking man) here.

Exercise 2.5: How Your Parents Saw You/
How You See Yourself

How my parents saw me

Abilities:
_____

_____

_____

_____

_____

Qualities:
_____

_____

_____

_____

_____

Talents:
_____

_____

_____

_____

_____

Special interests:
_____

_____

_____

_____

_____

How I see myself

Abilities:
_____

_____

_____

_____

_____

Qualities:
_____

_____

_____

_____

_____

Talents:
_____

_____

_____

_____

_____

Special interests:
_____

_____

_____

_____

_____

Exercise 2.6: Realistic or Imaginary Limitations?

Physical limitations: _____

_____

_____

_____

Negative personality characteristics: _____

_____

_____

_____

Obstacles to attaining my short-term goals: _____

_____

_____

_____

Obstacles to attaining my long-term goals: _____

_____

_____

_____

The limitations or obstacles that I believe are influenced by the critical inner voice:

_____

_____

_____

_____

_____

Part II

Challenging the Critical Inner Voice

Part I described the basic theory underlying the critical inner voice and showed how it operates to lower your self-esteem and intensify your feelings of shame and guilt. In part II, the same theoretical approach is used to explain how these destructive thoughts operate to limit you in important areas of your adult life: in your career, your relationships, and your sexual life; how it seduces you into using painkillers such as drugs and alcohol to cut off feelings; and how it can make you feel down and depressed. In this section, methods and exercises are provided for combating these destructive thoughts and improving your life. In addition, the final chapter in this section provides suggestions for finding a good therapist, if you decide you want to further develop yourself with the aid of psychotherapy.

Chapter 3

How the Critical Inner Voice Interferes with Your Career

Pray that success will not come any faster than you are able to endure it.

—Elbert Hubbard

This chapter focuses on how the critical inner voice can interfere with your achieving satisfaction in your work and how it can prevent you from attaining your career goals. You will see how business leaders, employees, and people involved in creative projects can overcome limitations imposed by the voice and how they can develop further in their careers. By identifying the specific thoughts and attitudes that control nonproductive work habits, you will be better able to achieve the level of success and sense of fulfillment you desire in your work.

Many experts have devised various strategies to improve performance, increase efficiency in the workplace, and overcome obstacles that stand in the way of people's expressing themselves through creative work. Numerous books have been written offering guidelines for developing character traits that would help people attain their career goals. Yet these strategies tend to neglect fundamental causes, and therefore many people run into trouble when trying to follow these suggestions.

Why do so many people, in all areas of the business world, habitually function far below their capabilities? Examples of nonproductive working styles are countless and can be readily observed in business and industry. Why is it that employees who receive significant raises often become incompetent in performing the same tasks for which they were rewarded? It's a well-known fact that executives as well as their employees often react negatively to an unusual success by developing self-defeating habit patterns that undermine their achievements.

A common thread running through these examples points to an important truth about human behavior: we all exist in a state of conflict between what we would like to achieve and what we allow ourselves to accomplish. All of us have strong desires to find satisfaction and fulfillment in all aspects of life. It is important to reemphasize that these tendencies are part of the "real self." At the same time, we have tendencies to sabotage our successes and limit our achievements; these tendencies are manifestations of our critical inner voice. Without an awareness of the malicious attitudes toward ourselves and others that are part of our critical inner voice, we may act in ways that are against our own best interests. The extent to which our behaviors are controlled by this negative point of view determines the state of mind we exist in while at work, which, in turn, can significantly detract from the company's productivity.

How Your Defenses Limit You in Your Career

We have brought with us, from childhood, the original methods that we developed to defend ourselves and to cope with the world as we knew it. As adults, we find that these strategies are often not only unnecessary and ineffective, but that they are actually harmful, in that they limit us in our lives today. This is especially obvious in our professional lives. We will discuss a number of the most common (and dysfunctional) methods of operating that people bring with them to the workplace.

Success Threatens the Fantasy Bond

There are many people who have a fantasy of being successful in business, but they don't want success in reality. This is because actual achievement jeopardizes the fantasy bond, a process that they have been using since childhood as a substitute for what was missing in their early environment. As a result, they look to fantasy instead of reality for satisfaction.

For example, for two years, Andrea had maintained an exceptionally high level of success as a salesperson. At a special dinner, her company rewarded her with a gold watch. The next month her sales fell dramatically. Over the following months, they declined even further.

Andrea sought counseling to help her understand her trouble at work. She soon identified the critical inner voices that had been plaguing her since she received the watch: *"Now they're going to expect more work from you. You'll have to generate more sales, with higher profit margins. You'll never be able to keep up the pace. They sure made a mistake. You don't deserve anything. Just watch how you're going to fail. You can never live up to this!"*

Andrea recognized that listening to these self-attacks and believing these distorted views about her employers had stirred up the resentment and anger she had felt as a child when, in fact, much had been expected of her. Andrea's father had died when she was fifteen, and she had to work long hours at a job she hated in order to supplement the family's income. Her family never expressed appreciation for her sacrifice. The reality of getting the acknowledgment for her contribution to the company had destroyed a fantasy she had carried with her since her early years, a fantasy of someday being appreciated and rewarded. She had projected the old, familiar feelings of resentment onto her coworkers and bosses and acted out these feelings by holding back her performance. Attaining success in reality effectively interferes with any satisfaction or comfort we may have been getting from fantasizing or imagining success in the future.

Success and Vanity

Sometimes people take a real success and try to use it to compensate for feelings of low self-esteem. They use their achievements as a way to exaggerate their feelings of importance, to build themselves up—in effect, to feed their vanity. Instead of enjoying real acknowledgment from other people who compliment them on their success, they become involved in an internal process of praising themselves. This is what happened to Tom, who is one of the top salesmen in a large corporation:

When I was only twenty-four years old, I began to be very successful in sales. I was involved with a fast-growing company and was a pivotal figure there. At first, I was just going along doing my thing. I really didn't even realize exactly what I was accomplishing. When management recognized my record sales, I was staggered to be appreciated for my contribution to the company. I was also gaining the respect of my peers.

The first thing that happened after that is that I became anxious, very scared. It was an identity that I wasn't familiar with. I quickly turned what I was doing into a role. It's a difficult thing to explain, but all of a sudden I was acting the part of "Tom Who Is Successful" instead of being someone who was simply himself. The minute I got self-conscious, it turned into more of an image instead of a reality. I wasn't being me anymore. I was looking at myself from the outside.

Everyone I worked with became very uncomfortable with the role I was playing. I really pushed my coworkers and friends away. I was patting myself on the back all the time, giving myself a lot of praise instead of accepting it coming from anyone else. I was telling myself: *"You've really made it! Just look at how customers respond to you! You're really good at selling. It's amazing that you've gotten this far in such a short time. They should appreciate all you've done for the company."* It was all self-contained at that point. And eventually it led to my actually sabotaging my own success. I was so much into the image or role that the customers started reacting to me negatively as well. They stopped wanting to talk to me or order from me.

Tom became more involved in playing a role than in actually performing the tasks at hand. He was also looking to his associates to build up his vanity, to support his image of exaggerated self-importance. It is interesting to note that before Tom got into the role of being supersalesman, he had more energy and was more appealing on a personal level. People who are operating from a vain point of view are less functional, less energetic, and less attractive than when they are simply being themselves.

Retreating from Competition

People sometimes pull back from performing well at work or retreat from a well-earned success because they are afraid of competitive situations. The critical inner voice is especially prominent in these situations. Men and women, fearful of competing for a promotion or a position of leadership, may tell themselves: *"Watch out for him (her). You'd better not let him (her) know you're competing for that position."* In other words, many people who would otherwise advance are afraid of retaliation from their rivals.

Self-critical thoughts are nearly always triggered by direct competition with a rival. For example, one woman who cofounded a large architectural firm struggled with her tendencies to retreat in the face of competition. She often found herself becoming subdued and pulling back from expressing her opinions, especially in discussions with male financial officers and architects. She identified the voices that encouraged her to retreat in these situations, *"They don't want to listen to a woman. They're the experts. Architecture is a man's field. What do you know, anyway? They have much more experience than you. Just play it safe and keep your opinions to yourself."* Afterward, she had insight into the origins of her tendencies to give up power:

I know that the biggest thing that limits me is that it's hard for me to go past the limitations my mother established for herself. First of all, my mother was so submissive in relation to my father. Then when she got a job, she deferred to her boss and never stated her opinions.

Not only am I guilty about surpassing her, but I also must have picked up her view of men and feel afraid of them being angry at me if I get ahead. I'm getting the feeling that it is really *her* fear, not mine. I can see now how I've been imitating the way my mother acted in relation to men. Each time I've advanced in my career, it's been hard for me, because of feeling guilty in relation to surpassing her and being afraid that I was an imposter in a man's world. I've talked to other women and this has been true of them, too. For me, that kind of guilt and irrational fear are much bigger limitations than any obstacles that men might be putting in my way.

Playing the Victim

Playing the victim is often a sign that a person is refusing to be an adult at work. A victimized attitude is never appropriate for adults, because they actually have power in their lives. Employees often act out the passive victim role and complain that they are being exploited or treated unfairly without considering the possibility that they could effect a change or even ultimately find another job. Instead, they manipulate others through "negative power," which may be expressed through incompetence, childishness, tears, and other signs of weakness. The critical inner voices underlying negative power have a self-righteous tone and include many "shoulds": *"They shouldn't treat you like that. Why do you always have to work late? Your boss is so unfair. He only criticizes your work, he never praises a job well done. Why should you go out of your way to help him when he gets all the credit?"*

It is never functional to see yourself as a victim. It is a view that leads to your giving up personal power—that is, your ability to assert yourself or make constructive changes. To recognize whether or not you are playing this role, examine your reactions. Do you tend to complain to your coworkers about your workload or about how unreasonable and demanding your boss is? Do you often feel overwhelmed or blame others for your failures or mistakes? If you have this pattern, it may not be because your boss is so demanding or terrible, but because you have put yourself in the role of the helpless victim.

This pattern of thinking and behaving may well be worth investigating, especially if you are repeating it in job after job. You may be playing a part in creating the very situations you are complaining about. Think back over the past work situations you have been involved in. Did you have voices that made you feel victimized in these situations? How are these thoughts interfering in your current work situation?

In the world of work, to avoid feeling like a victim, develop initiative and learn to assert what control you can over the situation. If you are unhappy, you need to feel free enough within yourself to be able to speak up or, if the problem is recurring, to change jobs when you feel the situation cannot be remedied. This means that it is important for you to develop your own personal power—your own goals and priorities.

Exercise 3.1: Career Goals:
Your Critical Inner Voice/The Real You

Take some time to compose your vision of the ultimate career goal you have for the future. Then in exercise 3.1, on the left-hand side of the page, write a paragraph that states this goal in a way that has personal meaning for you. If you have not yet decided on a career, take a few minutes to reflect on what ideals and values have the most meaning to you in your life, then write a brief paragraph about the activities that express your ideals. If you already have a career, write a paragraph that captures the essence of your goals in that field. If you have more than one goal to which you are committed, write a brief statement about each additional goal. Then, in the middle column, write down how your critical inner voice attacks these goals. On the right-hand side of the page, list the realistic barriers you feel may stand in the way of your accomplishing your ultimate career goal or goals. Here are three examples of exercise 3.1:

My career goal(s)	What my critical inner voice says	My realistic thoughts
Student: I want to work with children, not just teaching them skills for living, but also inspiring them to be the best people they can be and teaching them about the pleasure and rewards that come from helping others.	*"What do you know about children—how they learn, what will inspire them? You don't have that much experience with children. What makes you think you'd be a good teacher?"*	Lack of money for graduate school to obtain my master's degree in education.
Computer programmer: My goal is to create a new software program that takes computer science to a new level of technological sophistication. I envision being recognized for my contribution by my peers and supervisors.	*"Who do you think you are, anyway? Einstein? All you really want is to be seen as a big shot by your friends."*	No free time at night to work on my own projects. No extra money to hire an assistant and lack of encouragement from my wife (husband).
Manager of design firm: My personal goal is my company's mission statement: to create aesthetically pleasing environments for our clients, to stay within budget, to complete installations on time, and to put serving the client's best interests above other considerations.	*"This sounds corny and stupid. No one believes that you can always finish a project on time. That's so unrealistic!"*	Challenge of how to motivate project managers to think ahead, plan well, and stay within budget and on schedule.

Wanting to Be Taken Care Of

The tendency to become overly dependent can also interfere with work success. To the extent that we want to be "taken care of," we will experience thoughts that go along with this attitude. We will tend to be concerned about getting approval and will rely on other people's opinions rather than developing our own. We may tell ourselves, *"Your boss is the one making the decisions. After all, he's the expert. Who do you think you are to set policy? Just figure out what you're supposed to do and do it!"* The critical inner voice may undermine your self-confidence and trust in your capabilities, which can lead to your depending on your coworkers or the boss for support, approval, and care.

This tendency can also be seen in people working at the management level. Most people in authority are reluctant to reveal any feelings of dependency and insecurity. They tend to deceive themselves and rationalize their demands to be taken care of by such thoughts as: *"You've delegated that job, now they should take care of it without any more direction from you."* The underlying meaning is: *"They should take care of you, that's their job."*

You can see how people's ability to function in a mature, responsible manner at work would be seriously compromised by these kinds of rationalizations, which are promoted by the inner voice. The goal for employees and managers alike is to give up dependent behaviors, move toward independence, and ultimately learn how to be interdependent—that is, to work in harmony with others rather than depending on them for approval or support.

Holding Back Your Work Performance and Positive Qualities

Perhaps the most costly behavior in terms of loss of productivity can be found in people's withholding behaviors, wherein they hold back or inhibit the positive qualities and talents they possess. These self-defeating behavior patterns may be expressed in many ways: through procrastination, fatigue, lack of concentration, disorganized or nonproductive working styles, forgetfulness, and incompetence. The cost to industry and business of withholding on the part of employees is immense.

There are two motivating factors that contribute to withholding behavior. First, a person cannot tolerate the positive change of identity involved in success, and reacts by becoming withholding, as Andrea did in the earlier example. Second, withholding can be used by employees as a way of dealing with anger and resentment in an atmosphere where outward expressions of anger are typically not tolerated. In this type of setting, angry feelings come out in passive ways that irritate and provoke employers.

Lynne McClure, in her book *Anger and Conflict in the Workplace* (2000), described this type of "undercover anger" as being a "behind the scenes" anger, resulting in behaviors that are disruptive in work situations. According to McClure, many people are completely unaware that these actions are expressing an underlying anger, and so they feel innocent if they are accused of being incompetent or inefficient.

Typical Withholding Behaviors in the Workplace

Because patterns of withholding are often unconscious and are expressed primarily in passive behaviors, they may be difficult to identify and confront directly. A team of managers was asked to list actions and communications in the workplace that provoked them, or in their own words, "literally drove them crazy." Under the heading "Employees," their list included: the secretary who habitually forgets to convey phone messages; the accountant who is late issuing payroll checks; the warehouse worker who ships the wrong equipment; people who appear to be extremely busy, yet accomplish very little; and employees who take two-hour lunches, spend hours browsing the Internet, or use office time making personal calls or gossiping about coworkers. Under the heading "Fellow Managers," they listed: disorganization; excessive and unnecessary business meetings; failure to be a "team player"; inability to prioritize goals and steps toward goals; a habit of putting down associates to build themselves up; poor communication skills; reluctance to share information; and a disrespectful attitude toward salespeople and other employees.

Identifying Specific Voices That Govern Withholding Behaviors

Because most withholding behaviors are driven by unconscious forces, it is understandable that we often feel wounded and misunderstood or angry and defensive when we receive feedback about being withholding. We can make important inroads, however, by becoming aware of these self-defeating patterns in ourselves and attempting to identify the thoughts that are causing us to sabotage our successes.

The story of Brad is an example of the type of withholding that is motivated by the fear of changing our basic image of ourselves. Throughout Brad's childhood, his father started several businesses, but each one failed in turn. Although Brad often helped out in his father's businesses, his parents saw him as lazy, inconsiderate, and aloof. They continually told him he would never amount to anything.

Despite his parents' negative perceptions of him, Brad became an outstanding attorney, with a specialty in corporate law. His knowledge of finance and business practices was also well developed. As a consultant to a failing company, Brad was instrumental in turning it around and transforming it into a flourishing enterprise. As a result, he was hired as the company's new CFO. However, several months after assuming the position, he began missing executive meetings and failing to return phone calls and e-mails, and he seemed indifferent to the day-to-day activities of the company. Other members of the executive committee and employees alike complained about his behavior. Even more alarming, the company developed a serious cash flow problem and Brad's job was on the line.

Puzzled by his behavior, Brad sought counseling about the crisis he was facing at work. He identified the critical inner voices that were contributing to his holding back the very behaviors that had earned him the position of CFO:

> I felt like I was going out on a limb taking over this position. I felt demoralized by the kinds of things I was telling myself, like: *"What makes you think you can be any different from me? How can you manage a company? You're so incompetent and lazy. Besides, you're not the kind of person who leads people. You were always a cold fish. You don't know how to treat people. You're so inconsiderate. It's such a joke! You think you can handle the finances of a huge company? You can't even manage your own time!"*

After identifying the sarcastic, derisive attitudes he had toward himself, Brad realized that instead of experiencing the fear and anxiety he felt immediately after he was made CFO, he had gradually reverted to acting in ways that fit in with how his parents had defined him. By holding back his performance, Brad was attempting to reduce his fear of changing the negative identify he had formed in his family.

The story of Trish is an example of withholding that is motivated by underlying anger. Trish had been on the faculty of a large university for over ten years. The head of her department hired a renowned male researcher (at a high salary) to increase the university's ability to attract large grants. Soon, Trish found herself performing far below her own standards, failing to show up for class on time, and procrastinating on writing her own grant proposals. She realized that she was angry at the chairman of her department. In a journal she kept, she began to write down her critical inner voices. The negative thoughts she recorded expressed her jealousy, envy, and desire to get even with the department chair for hiring someone toward whom she felt highly competitive. These were some of the thoughts she listed: *"Why does he make twice as much money as you? You've worked here ten years. Your department chair is crazy. He has no appreciation for how much you've done. He doesn't recognize how much you contribute to the department and all the money you've brought in, or he wouldn't have hired him. You should just quit. Why work so hard when you're not appreciated?"* Writing down these critical inner voices gave Trish considerable relief and she began to realize her anger was exaggerated. As a child, she had been intensely rivalrous with her brothers because her parents had clearly favored them over her and her sisters. Recognizing that much of her anger was misplaced, Trish recovered her energy and enthusiasm for her teaching and research.

Becoming Aware of Withholding Behaviors and Their Underlying Voices

The first step in learning about withholding patterns of behavior that interfere with your achieving satisfaction and fulfillment at work is to make a list of those that you are able to identify in yourself. Although you may not be consciously withholding your best performance, you may be able to identify behaviors that you engage in that are examples of withholding.

Exercise 3.2: Withholding Behaviors: Your Critical Inner Voice/The Real You

On the left-hand side of the page in exercise 3.2, write down the behaviors that you believe are the most harmful to your succeeding at work. Then, in the middle column, describe what your critical inner voice says about each behavior. This could include thoughts about your work and your coworkers that are interfering with your achieving your goals at work. On the right-hand side, write down how you realistically view the withholding behavior.

Example of exercise 3.2:

Withholding behaviors	What my critical inner voice says	My realistic thoughts
I am often late for work.	*"What's the big deal? It's only 10 or 15 minutes. Other people are late."*	Being on time means something. It shows that I take my job seriously.

Where Does Withholding Come From?

The second step in taking power over the voices that influence withholding behaviors is to develop an understanding of when and where these behaviors began. To varying degrees, we all have tendencies to hold back our performance or our positive qualities and talents, and these withholding habit patterns began in childhood. As children, when we felt angry in relation to the pain we experienced, it is likely that our angry feelings were unacceptable and we had to suppress them. However, we found indirect ways of dealing with this anger. Children soon discover that by not performing—by not doing what their parents want—they are able to exert a considerable influence. When we indirectly acted out anger toward our parents or other authority figures such as teachers, we felt some measure of relief. Another cause of withholding can be a response to situations where parents want their children to succeed not so much for the sake of their children's happiness, but so that the parents can feel good about themselves. This kind of pressure makes it difficult for us to separate our own wants from those of our parents.

Many parents contribute to the development of withholding patterns in their children by underestimating their offspring's capability and readiness to accept responsibility. They fail to teach their children to be productive in the home environment and discourage their participation in more important functions as they grow older. Many of us have become so accustomed to withholding that we may actually believe we are unable to perform certain tasks that are, in reality, within our capabilities.

In addition, if our parents withdrew from success and were failure-oriented, we may find ourselves imitating them. Parents are often not aware that their own attitudes toward work are paramount in providing good role models for their children's later success in their chosen career. Parents who complain about their jobs or bosses and who feel victimized impart this attitude to their children. Some parents who are driven to overwork see their value only in what they accomplish, and often their children imitate their compulsive work patterns. On the other hand, parents who take pride in their career and approach their work with energy and dedication reinforce positive attitudes toward work in their children.

How Social Pressure Operates in the Workplace

Negative social pressure from supervisors and coworkers often acts to reinforce destructive thoughts that urge us to hold back our top performance—to not even try to do our best. For example, a man hired to package and load computer terminals onto trucks for shipping was warned by his coworkers not to load more than a certain number per day. They were worried that their performance would suffer by comparison.

In this particular case, social pressure to perform below a given level was out in the open. The new employee was aware of the threat implied by the others in his department. Given this awareness, he was able to decide whether to give in to their intimidation and slow down his performance to the "acceptable" quota, or to continue working up to his own standards.

When social pressure is verbalized or otherwise explicit, we can choose whether to conform to established standards or to strive for excellence. However, in the case of implicit social pressure, the intimidation is subtle or unspoken, and therefore more effective. This type of social pressure operates to arouse our fears and guilt reactions on a level that is not fully conscious. In addition, people's tendencies to conform to group standards and sanctions rather than stand out from the crowd operates to reinforce this form of social pressure.

Most people have a tendency to identify with leaders and imitate their behaviors. For example, if a boss shows by her action that the customer doesn't come first, even though she pays lip service to the principle, the salespeople and customer service personnel throughout the company often act accordingly and fail to give the customer the highest consideration and quality service. An angry, domineering manager may find that his harsh style has become part of his employees' behavior pattern. In general, workers adopt the same attitudes and behaviors in their interactions with coworkers and customers that their employer displays toward them.

Identify and Overcome Voices That Interfere with Your Creativity

If your work involves creating a product or expressing yourself through writing, music, art, or drama, it is possible that you are especially vulnerable to the influence of your critical inner voice. In the process of creating, you are expressing your own unique point of view, your real self; therefore, self-attacks arising from the opposing point of view, the critical inner voice, are likely to occur. Creative tasks usually involve blocks of time alone for concentrated work, and extended periods of isolation inevitably give rise to the critical inner voice. For example, a writer might find himself or herself thinking: *"This sounds so trivial. It's totally dull and boring. Just delete it and start over again. Whatever made you think you could write in the first place? What were you trying to prove? All you've proved is that you don't know the first thing about the subject or about writing!"*

In each area where we attempt to express ourselves through a creative medium, we are exposing ourselves to voice attacks. When people appear in public, are interviewed on the radio, or perform on stage or in front of the camera, voices can intrude and interrupt the performance. For example, an actor might find himself or herself thinking: *"You're too stiff. Do something with your hands. You look so weird and awkward. See, the director is scowling at you. You look like a wooden soldier and you're supposed to look natural! This is such a joke, you trying to be an actor. Face it, you just can't do it. You just don't have what it takes!"*

When you are engaged in a creative project, you can use the following exercise to identify the thoughts that are interfering with your progress.

Exercise 3.3: Creative Projects: Your Critical Inner Voice/The Real You

At the top of the page in exercise 3.3, fill in "The goal of my project." On the left-hand side of the page, write down specific steps necessary to complete the project. Next, in the middle column, write down how your critical inner voice is attacking you and interfering with your progress. On the right-hand side, write your realistic appraisal of how you are progressing.

Exercise 3.4: The Firestone Voice Scale for Work

Filling out this scale can help you identify some of the voices you have that are interfering with your work life. The scale includes voices that contribute to vanity and withholding behavior, and to retreating from competition, playing the victim, wanting to be taken care of. Becoming more familiar with your critical inner voices in relation to work can help you realize what patterns of behavior you may be engaging in that are interfering in your career.

In this chapter the question has been raised: what is standing in the way of your achieving your career goals? At times we find ourselves behaving in a self-defeating manner in the workplace just as we do in our personal lives and relationships. However, in many instances, we may not be aware that we are imposing certain limitations on ourselves at work and may find ourselves blaming a failure or a mistake on external events or on other people.

This chapter explains the destructive thoughts that are behind these difficulties. When we "listen" to the critical inner voice, we usually end up sabotaging our highest ambitions and often turn away from a hard-won success. Once the link between the critical inner voice and nonproductive work habits is understood, a number of steps can be taken to overcome these difficulties. You can use the methods and exercises in this chapter to improve your work habits and develop your ability to express yourself through creative work.

Our involvement in the world of work is essential to our achieving fulfillment, happiness, and a sense of well-being. Succeeding in our careers can enrich our lives, contribute to our independence, and provide us with the freedom to be able to enjoy all the other dimensions of life.

Exercise 3.1: Career Goals:
Your Critical Inner Voice/The Real You

My career goal(s)	What my critical inner voice says about my goal(s)	My realistic thoughts about my goal(s)

Exercise 3.2: Withholding Behaviors: Your Critical Inner Voice/The Real You

Witholding behaviors	What my critical inner voice says	My realistic thoughts

Exercise 3.3: Creative Projects:
Your Critical Inner Voice / The Real You

The goal of my project:

Steps to complete my project	What my critical inner voice says	My realistic thoughts
_____	_____	_____
_____	_____	_____
_____	_____	_____
_____	_____	_____
_____	_____	_____
_____	_____	_____
_____	_____	_____
_____	_____	_____
_____	_____	_____
_____	_____	_____
_____	_____	_____
_____	_____	_____
_____	_____	_____

Exercise 3.4: The Firestone Voice Scale for Work

Circle the frequency with which you experience the following critical inner voices about work:

0 = Never   1 = Rarely   2 = Once in a while   3 = Frequently   4 = Most of the Time

0 1 2 3 4   You're so bossy! Why should people listen to you?

0 1 2 3 4   You've organized the systems for the day-to-day operations, now other people should be able to carry them out without bothering you.

0 1 2 3 4   Why should anyone take orders from a woman?

0 1 2 3 4   You're an imposter. You don't know what you're talking about.

0 1 2 3 4   Why do *you* always have to work late? Why does all the extra work seem to fall on *you*?

0 1 2 3 4   Your boss is a jerk! He doesn't give a damn about you or his other employees, so why should you help him meet his quota this month?

0 1 2 3 4   Who do you think you are? You're way out of line. No one in your family ever got this far up the ladder of success.

0 1 2 3 4   You're going to go far in this job because you've got more business know-how than anybody else in the company.

0 1 2 3 4   You can't handle a career *and* a family. Look, your mother stayed home with you, so what makes you think that *you* can do both?

0 1 2 3 4   You've got to do more research before you start writing. You don't have anything new to say on the subject anyway.

0 1 2 3 4   You'll feel more like working on this project tomorrow. Besides, you've got other, practical things to take care of first.

0 1 2 3 4   You've wasted all this time writing and what have you got to show for it? A couple of pages and they're terrible, flat, weak, no power.

0 1 2 3 4   You've worked hard enough for today. It's time to take a break, get some coffee, go to lunch, have a drink.

0 1 2 3 4   You'd better be careful who you tell about your promotion. There's a lot of backstabbing going on around here.

0 1 2 3 4   You've got a lot of talent that's being wasted in this job. They just don't appreciate you here.

0 1 2 3 4   Now that you've got this position, they're going to expect a lot more from you. You're not going to be able to keep up the pace.

0 1 2 3 4   You are the only one here who knows how to do things right.

0 1 2 3 4   Working is such a drag.

0 1 2 3 4   Check your work—it better be perfect!

0 1 2 3 4   You have that show coming up, you will never get everything done.

0 1 2 3 4   You are such a fool to think anybody is going to like what you have created.

0 1 2 3 4   You are the best employee they have. They better hang on to you, and give you what you want.

0 1 2 3 4   Nobody likes you here. You should just quit this job.

0 1 2 3 4   You better put your career first. Work really hard or you will never get anywhere.

0 1 2 3 4   Why should you go to school? You will never succeed.

0 1 2 3 4   When are you ever going to get a real job and work hard for a change?

Chapter 4

How the Critical Inner Voice Influences Your Relationship

It is also good to love, because love is difficult. For one human being to love another human being: that is perhaps the most difficult task that has been entrusted to us, the ultimate task, the final test and proof, the work for which all other work is merely preparation.

—Rainer Maria Rilke

In no other area of life do we live out our negative destiny according to our past programming more than in our closest relationships. In associations that could be the most rewarding, we preserve the identity formed in our family and, in the process, push love away. This identity is often made up of negative fantasies and beliefs regulated by the critical inner voice. Changing our negative identity arouses considerable anxiety, and so, paradoxically, most of us try to maintain our negative self-image at all costs. Being close to another person in a loving relationship also makes us aware that life is precious, but must eventually end. If we embrace life and love, we must also face death's inevitability.

When we do take a chance and move toward fulfilling our personal goals in a relationship, we tend to experience varying degrees of anxiety. If we challenge our fears and learn to tolerate being loved, we can hold on to the territory we have gained. On the other hand, if we refuse to take a chance on being vulnerable in a relationship and instead retreat to a defended posture, we unintentionally punish those who love and respect us. We behave in ways that modify the loving feelings of our partners so that they eventually come to see us as we see ourselves—in a negative light. Most people remain unaware of this important dynamic in relationships.

The goal in this chapter is to help you recognize the voice attacks that may be generating conflict, distance, or dissatisfaction in your relationship. By identifying specific self-attacks, as well as hostile, judgmental thoughts about your partner, you can learn to relate more openly to your loved one. In revealing the contents of your voice attacks and following the corrective suggestions described in the second part of the chapter, you can begin to interrupt patterns of dishonest communication that may exist in your relationship. These guidelines and exercises can also facilitate deeper levels of communication between you and your partner.

How the Critical Inner Voice Interferes with Intimacy

The primary reason relationships fail is that each partner brings to the relationship his or her own critical inner voices and the defensive behaviors these voices regulate. In troubled relationships, both partners are often "listening" to the dictates of their voices. In a sense, their communications are being filtered through a negative point of view that distorts the way they view themselves and their partners. Both parties tend to push away loving responses from the other and use rationalizations promoted by the voice to justify their anger and distancing behaviors. In addition, they tend to project their own self-criticisms onto one another and react as though they were being criticized by their mates.

Many of us are influenced by voice attacks that deprecate or ridicule the pursuit of love. We "listen" to voices that warn us against becoming emotionally invested in caring for another person. For example, if you begin to feel loving responses toward a new partner, you may find yourself thinking: *"Watch out! Don't get too involved"* or *"Why should you care about him (her)?"* or *"Wait! Do you really like him (her) that much? Put on the brakes, things are going too fast"* or *"You're such a sucker to believe that real love exists."* Sometimes cynical or suspicious voices about other people predict future rejection or hurt: *"You're just going to get rejected in the end. Men (women) are all alike, they'll just toss you aside sooner or later. They don't really care!"*

When we learn to ignore the dictates of these seemingly self-protective voices, we discover that the attacks labeling us as foolish for loving and trusting another person are not at all logical or accurate. We realize that the act of loving someone else brings its own reward, because it feels good. We also find that caring for and being generous toward our partner enhances our positive feelings for ourselves.

How the Fantasy Bond
Works in Relationships

Generally speaking, the single most important factor that contributes to the deterioration of love and friendship in a relationship is the formation of a fantasy bond. People who develop this type of destructive bond often deceive themselves and each other by imagining that they still love each other long after their feelings of love, affection, and friendship have diminished or disappeared altogether. Understanding the concept of the fantasy bond helps answer questions that all of us have asked at one time or another: "Why did this love affair die?" or "Why did this marriage fail?"

Statistics show that about 50 percent of marriages end in divorce, that the average marriage lasts only seven years, and that approximately one-half of those who are married say they are dissatisfied and unhappy. Yet it is also a fact that most people still see a harmonious marriage as the ideal for which to strive. Why is there such a discrepancy between people's actions and what they claim to want most out of life? One reason is that most people don't really want what they say they want, as noted in chapter 3. In fact, many people seem to find it easier to fantasize about love than to tolerate the real experience of being loved. For example, most partners say they love each other; however, if you observe them closely you'll find it difficult to reconcile their behavior with any reasonable definition of the word "love."

Why is it that many people find comfort and security in fantasy and turn away from the real satisfaction and happiness they could have in genuinely loving relationships? The answer lies in childhood. As described in chapter 1, all children, to varying degrees, suffer emotional pain and anxiety in the process of growing up. In families where the parents are unable to provide the love and affection as well as the direction and guidance necessary to meet their child's needs or to enhance his or her development, the child forms an illusion of being at one with the mother or primary caregiver as a substitute for what is missing in the environment. Children develop a false sense of being totally self-sufficient by relying on this fantasy to partly relieve their pain, anxiety, and hunger. They feel as though they are a complete system within themselves, made up of the nurturing parent and the needy child.

The more seriously deprived or rejected we were as children, the more we tend to create this fantasy and believe that we need no one but ourselves. Later, as adults, we resist real closeness and genuine love from other people and are reluctant to take another chance in an intimate relationship. We are afraid that if we take the risk, we will be exposed to the same depth of anxiety, fear, and emotional pain that we were trying to escape when we originally formed the fantasy bond, at a time when we were helpless and dependent. So we form a fantasy of being close and loving, of being connected to our partner, just as we imagined we were connected to our parents. We repeat the patterns of the past and avoid taking a chance on having a real relationship with another person. It seems that many people would rather repeat the same pattern, which feels familiar and somehow safe, than take a chance on something new.

In summary, the fantasy bond, which originally was an imagined connection to our parents, later is extended to the outside world in the form of an addictive attachment or an overdependency on a person in our adult life. This external part of the fantasy bond is supported by signs that we "belong" to our partner and by other symbols that reinforce a pretense of love. However, a relationship in which both partners have formed this imaginary tie may have very little real intimacy, warmth, or affection.

How the Critical Inner Voice and the Fantasy Bond Work Together to Destroy Relationships

Feelings of self-depreciation as well as distrust of others protect the fantasy bond and support our feelings of being self-sufficient—our belief that we don't need anybody. If we are suspicious of other people or feel badly about ourselves, we will tend to have difficulty reaching out to others and will depend more on ourselves and on a variety of self-soothing activities. For example, you may feel more relaxed spending time alone reading or watching TV rather than responding to an invitation from friends to join them at a social function. Or you may not actively seek out situations where you could meet someone new, but instead may limit your social contact to one or two people you have known for years. Our fantasies of being rejected, negative expectations about relationships, and a cynical view of others are all maintained by the critical inner voice and its destructive point of view.

Whenever people are acting on their critical inner voice—that is, basing their actions on a hostile view of themselves and the world—their interactions with others tend to be angry, intrusive, or objectionable. Both forms of negative thinking—about ourselves and about others—support the fantasy bond and lead to alienation in relationships. For example, if you see yourself as deficient or unlovable, or if you are cynical and distrust other people, you are less likely to pursue love or to seek satisfaction in a relationship. As a result, when we encounter someone who genuinely acknowledges and loves us, we begin to feel anxious. We experience discomfort, emotional pain, and sadness because the positive view of ourselves conflicts with our negative self-image and the defenses with which we are familiar. At these times, the critical inner voice may become stronger and more insistent, telling us that we don't deserve love, or it may point out and exaggerate any flaws or weaknesses in the person who loves us.

Signs of a Fantasy Bond in Your Relationship

How can you tell if you have begun to form a fantasy bond in your relationship? What should you look for? One early sign is that the contact between you and your partner is less close and intimate and more superficial and routine. There is diminished eye contact between you. Your style of communication tends to become less personal and is characterized more by small talk, bickering, speaking for each other, interrupting, or talking in terms of "we"—"This is how *we* do things, this is what *we* think." Where you once spent hours in conversation, you may begin to lose interest in both talking and listening. Spontaneity and playfulness gradually disappear.

Have you fallen into a routine way of making love, and do you experience less sexual desire for and attraction to your partner? This decline is not necessarily the result of familiarity, as many people assume. When one or both partners begin to sacrifice their individuality to become halves of a couple, the basic attraction each feels for the other declines.

As a fantasy bond develops and genuine loving behaviors are withheld, partners try to cover up this painful reality with a fantasy of enduring love, substituting form for the substance of the relationship. Everyday routines, customs, rituals, and role-determined (nonspontaneous) behavior replace the real friendliness and affection that have decreased or disappeared altogether. People now act out of a sense of obligation instead of a true desire to be together.

Despite the fact that there is less real personal feeling in a fantasy bond, threats to this imagined connection can bring out dramatic emotional reactions in one or both partners. For example, Dave and Eileen, married for fifteen years, had gradually drifted apart. For as long as Dave could remember, there had been animosity between them based on Eileen's living beyond their budget. The couple's sex life was nonexistent, and both partners had separate groups of friends. Because of their mounting debts, they finally had to sell their home, and Eileen moved in with her mother. Wishing to start over with a clean slate, Dave suggested to Eileen that they get a legal separation. Eileen responded by saying she wanted a divorce.

Later, Dave talked about his reaction to a friend. "The minute Eileen said the word *divorce*, my heart started racing and I turned pale. I felt terrified, in a total panic. What would I do without her? By the end of the conversation, I told her I had changed my mind and that we should keep on the way we had been going. I know I sold out, but I don't understand why. Why am I so shaken up? I still feel really depressed. Intellectually I know it's crazy, because we've had nothing together for years. It's not like I'd be losing anything if we got divorced, but I feel like I'd be losing my right arm."

Dave's overemotional reaction was based on the fact that he was losing the form of the relationship, rather than losing the real person, Eileen, from whom he had grown distant a long time before. Melodramatic responses such as these, which stem from the anxiety aroused when the couple's fantasy of love and closeness is disrupted, are often mistaken for genuine caring for each other.

A fantasy bond is often strengthened after partners have made a commitment to living together, to marriage, or to starting a family. They use these commitments as guarantees of continued love and security—external signs of a fantasy of connectedness. For people who have a poor self-image, this sense of "belonging" to another person, of being loved "for ever after," offers a reassurance that is hard to resist. On the other hand, for mature individuals, a mutual commitment that expresses each partner's desire to be associated with the other throughout life can be an indication of deep feeling instead of an attempt to find ultimate security.

Playing the Parent/Playing the Child

As a fantasy bond develops, people who originally related as equal adults may assume either a childish, dependent or parental, authoritarian role. For example, Barbara revealed in a couples' group how she gradually gave up her opinions and looked to her husband for direction after they married:

> The most painful thing in my relationship with Len is that I gradually gave up my point of view. When we first met, I was in college, I was planning my career, and I was very interested in politics. Len and I would have long conversations about everything—politics, religion, world affairs. He had very strong opinions and so did I, and I really enjoyed our discussions. But after we were married, or maybe even before that, I started thinking that he knew more than I did, that he was smarter than I was, and I submerged my opinions until I hardly knew anymore what I really thought or believed.

In some cases, women become more dependent and childlike and look to men to be taken care of. In other cases, men give up their point of view and look to women for definition and direction. Neither the child nor the parent role is a genuine reflection of the partners' real selves. The partner who is acting the parental role disowns feelings of fear and helplessness, just as the partner acting the child role denies feelings of power and competence. Each partner may complain about the childishness or bossiness of the other; however, they are usually reluctant to make any real changes and relate again from an equal, adult position. A move on the part of either partner toward genuine independence would disrupt the fantasy bond and generate strong feelings of anxiety in both individuals.

How We Defend Ourselves Against Love

An unfortunate truth about human beings is that very often the beloved is compelled to punish the lover. When someone sees us in a way in which we do not see ourselves, it threatens our defenses and disturbs the negative self-image we formed early in life. Most of us cling to these self-critical attitudes and are resistant to being seen in positive ways. We are reluctant to allow the experience of being loved to reach us on a level that would change our image of being unlovable or undeserving of love. Just feeling appreciated and loved for who we really are can bring out deep feelings of sadness and grief about what we may have missed early in our lives. Feeling loved also reminds us of how fragile and precious our life is, and we may experience a kind of anticipatory sadness about the future loss of our loved ones (and ourselves) through death.

Because we are afraid of feeling vulnerable, most of us retreat from being close and gradually, almost imperceptibly, give up the most valued aspects of our relationships. When our feelings of affection, sexual attraction, and friendship contrast with the unhappiness and rejection we experienced in the past, we unconsciously try to erase the difference.

Three Defenses

On a conscious level, we may believe we are looking for a loving relationship; however, on an unconscious level, all of us still tend to recreate the conditions within our original family in our present-day relationships. We do this in three ways: through selection, distortion, and provocation.

Selection

We tend to select partners who are similar to a parent, an older sibling, or another family member because we feel comfortable with them. We feel relaxed when our defenses are compatible with the defenses and style of relating of the mate we choose.

For example, Laura, a woman who much admired her father, a distant and unapproachable man, met Matt at a party and was immediately attracted to him. She said that he looked "lonely and a little sad, and that dreamy look in his eyes was just irresistible." She approached him as he stood alone on a balcony and struck up a conversation. They hit it off right away, and soon after began dating steadily. Initially, their attraction and sexual chemistry were intense. However, Laura began to feel rejected by Matt's preference for isolated activities and his preoccupation with work, and their sexual life suffered. Her complaints about Matt's ways of shutting her out only resulted in his further avoidance, and the couple eventually broke up. At the time they became involved, Laura was completely unaware of the similarity between Matt's distancing behaviors and her father's characteristic style of avoiding personal contact. In fact, the behavioral cues that would have warned Laura of Matt's preference for solitude were the very characteristics that had been so appealing to her when they first met.

What were Matt's early influences? The most important figure in Matt's early life was his mother. A highly intrusive woman, she demanded to know his every thought and feeling. She routinely met him at the door when he came home from school and insisted he sit down with her and tell her everything about his day. By the time Matt was a teenager, he had found ways to avoid her questioning by "spacing out," studying endlessly in his room, and imitating many of his father's ways of avoiding contact and family interactions.

When Matt met Laura at the party, he was strongly attracted to her friendliness and obvious interest in him. He was not at all put off by her questions about his life, with her asking what he thought and how he felt about a wide range of subjects. To the contrary, this trait was especially appealing to him. However, Matt grew to resent her endless inquiries and began to avoid conversations with her. His aloofness only made Laura more desperate for his attention. The couple became more and more polarized. They had no awareness that they had subconsciously set up the same conditions that had existed in each of their respective childhoods and were, in effect, reliving the past.

If you objectively look at the partners you have chosen in the past, what personal quality or trait drew you to them? Did some of their qualities or traits resemble any traits in one of your parents? In your current relationship, is there a particular behavior or quality in your partner that was especially attractive to you but that now irritates you?

Distortion

When we have selected a partner who is different from a parent in a significant way, we find ourselves in new, unfamiliar territory. However, we can relieve the tension and anxiety this causes us by distorting our partner—that is, by misperceiving him or her as similar to someone from our past. For example, Ellen's father was extremely critical of her and made sarcastic, derisive remarks about her. Ellen was fortunate in her choice of a partner. Bruce, her fiance, happened to be easygoing, and playful, and had a great sense of humor. He was not at all cynical or judgmental. When Bruce asked Ellen to marry him, she was thrilled. However, she soon began to distort the things he said to her, seeing them as critical statements and expressions of disapproval. In her mind, she twisted many of the good-natured, humorous remarks Bruce made about their relationship—remarks which in reality very much acknowledged her real self—and heard them as being sarcastic, disapproving, and critical.

Not all of our distortions are negative. We tend to see both the positive and the negative characteristics of a parent or sibling in new, significant people in our lives. Often, we may exaggerate a positive trait in a new partner and idealize him or her in the same way we idealized our parents. In addition, we may see our partner as stronger than he or she actually is because we want to be taken care of. When we do this, we may resent any signs of human weaknesses he or she displays.

Provocation

The third way we recreate our early family environment is to behave in ways that actually force familiar responses from our partners. By manipulating our mates, we can evoke the behaviors we are used to from our childhoods. Sometimes you can even provoke your partner to the point where he or she says aloud the same critical inner voices you have about yourself. These provocations often follow the most loving, tender moments between you and your partner, and thus create distance in your relationship.

For the most part, we are unaware of using these three maneuvers to defend ourselves from closeness and love. However, we may use these methods to transform a new relationship into one that more closely corresponds to the environment in which our defenses were formed and retreat to a more familiar, less vulnerable style of relating.

For example, as a child, Carl was seen as being irresponsible and was defined as a slacker or "flake" by his family. As a teenager, he assumed leadership roles in high school and was admired and respected by his peers, yet his family still saw him as a flake. As an adult, he went on to open a successful restaurant. Later, he met and married a woman who admired his integrity and strength. As the years went by, however, Carl became forgetful and irresponsible in managing his restaurant. On many occasions, his wife found herself being provoked by his lack of initiative and his passivity. At these times, their arguments would end with her calling him a "lazy, good-for-nothing flake." In effect, Carl had unconsciously recreated his past circumstances and reaffirmed the negative, yet familiar, identity formed in his family.

Suggestions for Disrupting the Fantasy Bond

There are several steps that you can take to break a fantasy bond if you have formed one with your partner and, in so doing, recapture some of the feelings of friendship and love you experienced initially in your relationship. You can:

1. Explore aspects of your relationship for signs of a fantasy bond. If you discover some indications, admit that they exist and stop avoiding the awareness that you have become distant and that your behaviors are no longer loving.

2. Admit you have critical, hostile voices toward yourself and your partner.

3. Face the emotional pain and sad feelings involved in trying to restore intimacy in your relationship.

4. Expose fears of being alone and separate, including fears of rejection, abandonment, loss or death of you or your partner.

5. Move toward independence and show respect for one another's goals and priorities.

6. Make every effort to establish equality in the relationship by breaking patterns of dominance and submission.

Exercise 4.1: The Firestone Voice Scale for Couples

Exercise 4.1 will help you identify specific voice attacks that may be influencing you in your relationship. You can use this scale to identify the voices you experience.

Exercise 4.2: You in Your Relationship: Your Critical Inner Voice/The Real You

On the left-hand side of the page in exercise 4.2, write the critical inner voices that you most often experience about yourself in your relationship. On the right-hand side of the page, record a more realistic view of yourself.

Exercise 4.3: Your Partner in Your Relationship: Your Critical Inner Voice/The Real You

On the left-hand side of the page in exercise 4.3, record negative thoughts that occur to you with the greatest frequency regarding traits and behaviors you dislike the most in your partner. These undesirable characteristics are often exaggerated by your inner voice. If you were to say these criticisms out loud, your tone of voice would probably take on a sarcastic, snide tone. Next, write down a more realistic or objective view of your partner on the right side of the page. You may notice that as you record these more positive views, the cynical or sarcastic attitude of this alien point of view toward your partner is diminished to a considerable degree.

Exercise 4.4: Relationships: Your Critical Inner Voice/The Real You

On the left-hand side of the page in exercise 4.4, write down any negative views you have about your relationship, or about relationships and marriage in general. Where do these views come from? From early experiences in your life? From the ways your parents related to each other? From the ways the media portrays relationships? From the ways you observe your married friends communicating and relating? Next, record what you realistically think about your relationship or relationships in general.

Learn to "Give Away" the Views of Your Critical Inner Voice

After you have become familiar with recording negative thoughts about yourself, your partner, and your relationship, you may wish to reveal them to your partner. Obviously, timing is important—your partner needs to be open to hearing some of the negative ways you have been thinking about him or her. You need to assure your partner that these voices do not represent your real point of view, but rather that they reflect hostile attitudes you learned early in life. Make every effort to remove the snide or sarcastic tone of these attacks on your partner and reveal the contents of these voices in a nondramatic style and with sensitivity to your listener.

You may want to have conversations in which you and your partner, in turn, disclose your self-attacks and hostile views of each other, while the other listens. Try to "give away" your critical inner voices in a nonblaming style, and attempt to not react to the critical voice statements of your partner as personal criticisms. In the process of sharing both our self-attacks and our cynical views of our partner with one another, we can develop the ability to listen to one another with understanding and compassion.

Most people feel relieved rather than personally attacked to hear their partners' negative statements spoken aloud. These are the same voices that their partners have been acting out rather than saying directly. In other words, one or both partners has already been suffering from these attacks. However, in the process of listening to their mates express the cynical, distrusting attitudes, the partners develop a clarity about what is really going on in the relationship, rather than remaining confused. They can begin to understand that the thoughts driving their partners' actions usually have nothing to do with them, but are based on projections from the past.

Talk with a Friend

Talk with a trusted friend at least twice a week for ten or fifteen minutes and reveal some of the critical inner voices you have about yourself and about your relationship. This will be especially valuable if you do not yet feel comfortable discussing these thoughts with your partner. The process of externalizing your inner voice exposes the content of this destructive thinking to the light of day, so to speak, and subjects it to reality testing. As a result, you will probably discover that many of the negative ways you've been thinking about yourself and your relationship are inaccurate. Some of your critical inner voices may even appear absurd or preposterous.

However, not all of the attacks on yourself are necessarily false. But even when there is some element of truth, it doesn't account for the strong hostility or viciousness toward yourself that usually accompanies these self-criticisms. The extremely hostile attitudes underlying your self-attacks must be separated from their content, even when the attacks reflect an objective reality. For example, what does your critical inner voice say about a negative quality you have identified in yourself? Now, what would an objective observer have to say about it? What would your friend say about it?

Identify Withholding Behaviors in Yourself

Identify any withholding patterns that you may have developed during the course of your relationship. There are literally hundreds of examples of withholding wherein we unconsciously hold back the positive personal qualities and behaviors that our loved ones particularly enjoyed or prized: our appearance or good looks, small acts of kindness, generous impulses, affection, and sexuality.

For example, a man told his new wife that she looked beautiful with long hair and that he loved the way it fell to her shoulders. The next week, on an impulse, she went to the hairdresser and had her hair cut extremely short. When she met her husband for dinner that evening, she was mystified by his look of shock and by the anger and disappointment he expressed.

In your relationship, it is important to not act out these witholding behaviors, because they can provoke anger in your partner. The following are directives from a humorous book by Patricia Love and Sunny Shulkin entitled *How to Ruin a Perfectly Good Relationship* (1997). Each statement represents a type of withholding behavior commonly observed in many couple relationships. It goes without saying that the objective here is to *not* engage in any of these behaviors, but rather to do the opposite:

> Make it a practice to be late. Be stingy with praise and appreciation. Withhold information. Let your partner hear the important details from someone else (like your mother or your secretary). Withhold sex (you get extra points for this one).
>
> Never let him (her) see you smiling. Exchange the gifts your partner buys for you. Deflect all compliments. Never ask for help. Refuse all of your partner's attempts to solve problems.
>
> Control everything and everyone. Hold fast to the belief: "If you loved me you would know what I want." When your partner tries to please you, find fault with the efforts. Keep no promises. Keep your true thoughts and feelings to yourself.
>
> Ignore your partner when he or she is sick or hurt. Pay more attention to the TV than your partner. Let days go by without a kind word or loving gesture. Take pleasure in withholding pleasure. Strike the words "I love you" from your vocabulary. Refuse to see how your partner shows you love.
>
> Refuse your partner's sexual overtures. Give up on sex. Decide you're just not sexual. Let passion die. Promise sex then don't follow through. Remain silent about your sexual needs but expect your partner to know what you want.
>
> And finally, "One-Liners Sure to Ruin a Relationship":

- To tell you the truth, I really don't enjoy touching that.

- I love you, but I'm not "in love" with you.

- I need to be alone on holidays.

Learn How to Give Up the Need to Always Be Right

Use the technique of "unilateral disarmament" to defuse escalating arguments. Angry exchanges between partners typically escalate from mild disagreements to outright hostility and verbal abuse. Yet, in many cases, it is relatively simple to interrupt the cycle of accusation and counteraccusation before one or both of you say or do something you later regret. At the moment you sense the disagreement is degenerating into a battle of wills, drop your stake in winning and reach out to your partner. You might say something warm and understanding, or stress that it doesn't really matter who is right, or express physical affection.

In general, positive expressions of caring in the midst of an argument are effectively disarming to the battling partner, who may feel touched by the other's gesture of peacemaking. As a result, the hostility often quickly dissipates. (It is difficult to maintain one side of an argument when the other has left the field of battle.) The technique of unilateral disarmament does not at all imply that you are surrendering your point of view or necessarily deferring to your partner's opinion. It simply indicates that you value being close to your partner more than winning your point.

Set Goals for Your Relationship

Remember that you have considerable power in your relationship. Although you have no power to change your partner, you have the power and ability to change yourself. Altering behaviors that are motivated by your critical inner voice will have the effect of modifying the dynamics and the interactions in your relationship.

For example, Janet decided that she wanted to be closer to her husband. For several weeks, her behaviors fit her goals. She treated him with more empathy and understanding, especially when he was under stress. Following her husband's three-day business trip, Janet phoned Carl at noon and suggested that they spend a romantic evening out on the town. Carl responded by saying that his day was going to be hectic because he had just returned and that he would much rather spend a quiet evening at home. Janet was disappointed and angry and began to feel that Carl was rejecting not only her proposal, but her as well. She told herself: *"If he really cared for you, he would certainly want to spend a romantic evening with you. He just doesn't appreciate you and all you've done for him!"*

During the afternoon, she felt cold and indifferent toward her husband from all the negative thoughts she was experiencing. She did not want to show any enthusiasm nor did she want to be vulnerable or want anything from him. Finally, she came to her senses. She realized that if she went with her first impulse and listened to her critical inner voice, she would be acting against her major goal, which was to be close to her husband. She decided to make a conscious effort to change her mood of irritation and indifference and be open to Carl when he came home, and to see what would develop. Carl was very affectionate from the moment he walked in the door. The couple spent a romantic evening in conversation, and their lovemaking seemed especially tender. Janet was struck by the realization that their evening might have been very different had she not chosen to act against her critical inner voices.

Exercise 4.5: Goals for Your Relationship

On the upper half of the page in exercise 4.5, record your goals for your relationship. On the lower half of the page, write down the actions you need to take in order to accomplish these goals. Keep track of your progress toward their attainment. Don't be discouraged if you find yourself wavering in the pursuit of your goals. Almost everyone slips back into old behavior patterns when they are under stress.

On a deep level, many men and women are frightened of genuine love and closeness. This leaves many of us dissatisfied, unhappy, and confused in our relationships. The source of this fear lies in the fantasy bond, the defense we formed early in life. We brought this way of protecting ourselves with us into adulthood, where it is no longer necessary. When we understand this and are able to identify and challenge the process that governs it—the critical inner voice—we can develop and sustain loving relationships.

Exercise 4.1: The Firestone Voice Scale for Couples

Circle the frequency with which you experience the following critical inner voices:

0 = Never   1 = Rarely   2 = Once in a while   3 = Frequently   4 = Most of the time

---

0 1 2 3 4   It's a man's job to take care of a woman.

0 1 2 3 4   You're never going to find another person who understands you.

0 1 2 3 4   Men are so insensitive. They're so opinionated. They don't want you to have your own views about anything.

0 1 2 3 4   Don't get too hooked on him (her).

0 1 2 3 4   You'd better give him (her) what he (she) wants.

0 1 2 3 4   Don't let him (her) know what you're thinking.

0 1 2 3 4   You always give in. You have no standards

0 1 2 3 4   Why get so excited? What's so great about him (her)?

0 1 2 3 4   You've got to build a man up, make him think he's really important.

0 1 2 3 4   Women are fragile, sensitive. You've got to be careful of what you say to them.

0 1 2 3 4   He (she) doesn't really care about you. If he (she) did, he (she) would show it more.

0 1 2 3 4   Don't be independent. Let him (her) take the lead.

0 1 2 3 4   What you feel and think isn't important to him (her).

0 1 2 3 4   You're a nobody! Who would care about you?

0 1 2 3 4   Don't ruin this relationship like the other ones.

0 1 2 3 4   He (she) is always with his (her) friends.

0 1 2 3 4   He (she) is too good for you. It would never work out.

0 1 2 3 4   You've got to keep him (her) interested.

0 1 2 3 4   Why isn't he (she) more affectionate?

0 1 2 3 4   Women are such a bother to deal with. They're childish and melodramatic, and they try to control everything.

0 1 2 3 4   You're too shy to meet new people. You're too self-conscious and awkward to talk to men (women).

0 1 2 3 4   You'd better not try for a really attractive woman (man). You're not good-looking enough.

0 1 2 3 4   You'd be better off on your own. You wouldn't have to put up with this crap!

0 1 2 3 4   No man stays with one woman forever. They're just not like that!

0 1 2 3 4   The next time he'll (she'll) find out what you're really like.

0 1 2 3 4   You're such an easy mark, a pushover.

0 1 2 3 4   You'd better get an education and a good job so you'll have something to fall back on when he leaves you.

0 1 2 3 4   You don't deserve love.

0 1 2 3 4   Sure, you're a fairly good-looking guy, but she's way out of your league, man.

0 1 2 3 4   You're so selfish. You want (expect) too much from a man (woman).

0 1 2 3 4   He can be such a jerk!

0 1 2 3 4   She can be such a bitch!

0 1 2 3 4   He (She) is always jealous. Why doesn't he (she) just grow up?

0 1 2 3 4   It's your own fault you get treated like this. You're always wanting too much, needing too much, asking for too much.

0 1 2 3 4   No wonder he (she) stood you up. He (she) had second thoughts.

0 1 2 3 4   Once he (she) gets to know you, he (she) will find out what you're really like.

0 1 2 3 4   You'd better put up a good front. Put your best foot forward or he (she) won't be interested.

0 1 2 3 4   You feel things too much. You're too vulnerable. You're going to get hurt.

0 1 2 3 4   Women don't understand the practical things in life.

0 1 2 3 4   Men don't care about feelings. They don't care about women and they don't care about children.

0 1 2 3 4   Before he (she) met you, he (she) was much better off. You're just a drag on him (her).

0 1 2 3 4   You've got to be in control. One wrong step and you'll end up alone.

0 1 2 3 4   Just find out what he (she) wants and go along with it. Things will go smoother.

0 1 2 3 4   You'd better get a good job and make a lot of money so you can support her (him).

0 1 2 3 4   He's a loser. He has no future. Don't get involved with him.

0 1 2 3 4   Don't let your feelings show. Don't let him (her) know that you really care. Play it cool.

0 1 2 3 4   No one will ever want you. You're going to end up old and alone.

0 1 2 3 4   He (she) doesn't really care about you.

0 1 2 3 4   All he (she) cares about is his (her) independence. What about you? Where do you fit into his (her) life?

0 1 2 3 4   You're not going to get along. You never do.

0 1 2 3 4   Women are not direct. They're not straightforward. They always change their minds.

0 1 2 3 4   You're responsible for how she (he) feels. If she (he) gets upset, it's your fault. You'll be blamed.

0 1 2 3 4   You've got to find a man, then keep him under control, because you need him to take care of you.

0 1 2 3 4   You're not much fun anyway. What do you have to talk about?

0 1 2 3 4   You don't need love anyway. You're strong.

0 1 2 3 4   Make him (her) feel that he's (she's) important, that you need him (her).

0 1 2 3 4   Why doesn't he (she) give a little bit more to the relationship?

Exercise 4.2: You in Your Relationship:
Your Critical Inner Voice/The Real You

What my critical inner voice says about me in my relationship

What I realistically think about myself in my relationship

Exercise 4.3: Your Partner in Your Relationship: Your Critical Inner Voice/The Real You

What my critical inner voice says about my partner in my relationship

What I realistically think about my partner in my relationship

Exercise 4.4: Relationships:
Your Critical Inner Voice/The Real You

What my critical inner voice says about relationships

What I realistically think about relationships

Exercise 4.5: Goals for Your Relationship

Goals I have for my relationship:

_____

_____

_____

_____

_____

_____

_____

Actions to take to achieve my goals:

_____

_____

_____

_____

_____

_____

_____

Chapter 5

How the Critical Inner Voice Intrudes on Your Sexual Relationship

When Eros comes in the door, very often love flies out the window. Bedrooms are among the most dangerous places on earth.

—R. D. Laing

Sex is a vital part of our experience as human beings and a strong motivating force in our lives. It has the potential for creating intense pleasure and fulfillment or causing much pain and suffering. A good deal of our misery is centered on sexuality and the difficulties we run into when we attempt to achieve and sustain sexual satisfaction, especially in a close personal relationship.

Our feelings about our bodies, the acceptance of our sexual identities as men and women, and our experiences with sex are fundamental to our sense of well-being and self-esteem. If we have a generally healthy orientation to sex, it is reflected in our level of vitality and our overall appearance. Disturbances in our natural sexuality can have serious consequences and can affect many aspects of our lives, including activities and pursuits far removed from our sex lives. The combination of loving sexual contact and genuine companionship in an intimate relationship contributes to mental health in general and is an ideal for which many people strive.

However, if we are viewing ourselves through the distorted lens of the critical inner voice, we may feel guilty about this natural and pleasurable part of life. To varying degrees, most of us learned inaccurate and unhealthy views of sex during childhood. Often we are unaware that, as adults, our views about sex are still being influenced by our past experiences and by these destructive thoughts and attitudes.

For example, have you ever wondered why, in this age of sexual enlightenment, direct conversation about sex is still considered by many people to be improper? Or why many people laugh nervously when the subject comes up? Why are jokes about sex considered dirty? Why is our sexuality such a matter for secrecy? Although there has been some improvement in societal acceptance of adult sexuality since the sexual revolution of the 1960s, nevertheless many people still have distorted views of sex that make them feel awkward or bad in relating to others a good deal of the time.

Two Views of Sex

Sex can have either a positive or a negative effect on our sense of self and on our ability to enjoy a mature and long-lasting personal relationship. The effect it has largely depends on how we look at sex and how we view ourselves as men and women. Just as we have two opposing points of view about ourselves, our partners, and our relationships, we also have two opposing views about our bodies and our ability both to give love and sexual satisfaction to our partner or mate and to receive them.

From a healthy, "clean" point of view, sex is a natural extension of affectionate feelings, rather than an activity separate from other parts of a relationship. Making love is an important form of communication, a way of giving and receiving pleasure. When we are thinking of sex in these terms, our sexual encounters may be playful, fun, sensuous, emotional, affectionate, serious, carefree, or a combination of these, depending on our mood.

In contrast, from an unhealthy or "dirty" point of view, sex is an activity that should be kept hidden and secretive; the human body is seen as shameful and those parts having to do with sexual functions are given a dirty connotation. From this perspective, sex is an activity that is completely separate from the rest of life. When sex is viewed in this light, it is seen as a subject unfit for social conversation or discussion, especially with children.

On an intellectual level, we would all agree that sexual functions are a simple and natural part of our makeup as human beings. However, on an emotional level, nearly every person in our society retains shameful feelings about his or her body. This has led to a variety of sexual problems and fears about sexual performance. These sexual problems exist on a continuum ranging from those that are mild in nature to serious disturbances in sexual relating. Distorted attitudes about sex that we learned or acquired from our parents, relatives, peers, and society often have a crippling effect on our sexuality and on our relationships in general. These attitudes, which take the form of the critical inner voice, can intrude into our thinking at any point during a sexual experience. These negative thoughts can have a detrimental effect on our ability to achieve satisfaction in the most intimate part of our relationships.

How Our Attitudes Toward Sex Are Influenced by Parents, Peers, and Society

Our negative attitudes toward sex usually reflect what our parents thought and felt about sex, about each other, and about men and women in general. Even though our parents may have been intellectually enlightened about sex, we could not help but take on their emotional attitudes, which may have been negative and distorted. In observing our parents, we could see how they treated each other, whether they were affectionate and warm or cool and aloof in their interactions.

In many families, parents rarely show signs of sexuality or indicate in any way to their children that they enjoy an active sexual relationship. Many people can remember, for instance, their parents sleeping in separate beds or bedrooms. Some parents are reluctant to express physical affection in front of their children. Others may make off-color jokes about sex or sneer at couples who do express affection in public.

Although many parents say that their children *should* learn healthy attitudes about sex, very few discuss sex openly and personally with their own children. Some mothers and fathers refuse to allow their teenage children to attend sex education classes, for fear they will be wrongly influenced to have sex. Others insist that the classes teach abstinence only and not include information about birth control or discussions about disease prevention.

Attitudes Toward Our Bodies

One indication of how we feel about sex is how we feel about our bodies. It is clear that infants and young children enjoy a sense of freedom and a lack of self-consciousness about being naked. By the time they are five or six, however, most children are deeply embarrassed to be seen without clothes. Many children pick up basic attitudes from their parents about nudity and the human body that intensify their feelings of self-consciousness.

In some families, the parents' general style of relating is overly sexualized. This can be as damaging as the restrictions placed on sexuality in families that are more rigid and suppressive. Kathy remembers:

Everything was sexual in my mind from when I was very young. And my parents didn't have any qualms about telling me about sex. I remember that one of my books when I was a little girl was about *Where Do I Come From?* and another one was called something like *I'll Show You Mine If You Show Me Yours.*

I think that in my family everything was sexual—I mean everything—and I think that I was treated that way. I remember that my father and mother would go out into the field with the whole family, and he would take pictures of her naked in the field. One of the pictures he took of my mother was hanging in the living room, showing her from the shoulders up, but I felt funny about it. It was like a secret thing to me that she was naked in the rest of the picture.

I thought that every interaction between a man and woman was a sexual interaction. I know that's how my parents felt, and that's how I thought, too. I never thought of friendship or of friendliness or even just affection. Sex was the beginning and the ending point—it was the only thing in life, that was how I saw things.

Attitudes About Masturbation and Sex Play

Over the past fifty years, attitudes about masturbation have changed considerably, yet many parents still react dramatically, on an emotional level, when they find their children masturbating. Parents' overreactions to masturbation can make the child feel guilty. As a result, the child learns to be secretive about this activity.

Just as children like to explore their own bodies, they also enjoy exploring and touching each other. Their natural curiosity about the differences between the sexes leads them to initiate sex play with siblings and playmates. Often when parents discover children involved in sexual play, such as games like "doctor and nurse," they reprimand them. However, children's interest in their own bodies and sexuality is a normal part of growing up. Parents can tell their children in simple terms that it is natural for them to be curious about themselves in this way. However, they could also point out that acting on their curiosity in public will usually be frowned on. A calm, nonjudgmental attitude on parents' part will support a child's developing healthy sexuality, including feelings of love and friendship.

Society's Attitudes About Sexuality

Distorted attitudes toward sexuality learned by people in their formative years combine to influence cultural attitudes and social mores. Societal institutions, rules, and restrictions then reflect back on each member of society in the form of negative social pressure. These cultural attitudes and standards invade every area of our daily lives and, more often than not, have a destructive effect on our sexuality.

Society's attitudes about sexuality often exert a negative social pressure on children's relationships with their peers. In a seminar on society's attitudes toward sex, Linda described an incident where her actions were misunderstood and ridiculed by her peers, who gave a dirty connotation to her friendship with a classmate:

> When I was in the fourth grade, there was this boy I really liked and we were really good friends. We would do everything together. We were best friends. One day we decided we were going to kiss each other. But it was like a big thing to be at all affectionate or anything like that.
>
> That day, we rode on his bicycle down to these woods and then to this big gravel pit. And we were sitting on the side of the gravel pit. We were very shy, so we were just talking about kissing, whether we were going to do it or not. But there were some boys from school in the woods and they heard us. So they came out of the woods and started ridiculing us and saying that we were going to be sexual. And I remember that both of us were traumatized from that. So we got on his bicycle and he rode me home and I remember he was crying. I felt so bad.
>
> Then the next day, these boys were saying all this stuff about us at school. It's like I died from humiliation, and so did he. But the worst thing was that from then on we never spoke to each other. It was so painful because we went through all the grades together and always saw each other. I even saw him at the senior prom. We came face to face at the senior prom and we couldn't even say anything to each other then.
>
> I can't even think about it today without remembering him crying on the way home, because his feelings were hurt. It seems like such a small incident, but it's such a terrible story, the fact that we didn't even speak to or look at each other after that.

A major function that families serve is to socialize children, that is, to teach them the standards and mores of the culture in which they live. However, many parents, in trying to impart good values to their children, fail to understand their children's emerging feelings of sexuality and are often insensitive in their comments to them about sex. In the same seminar, Ronald described how his mother's remarks made him self-conscious and later on affected him in his adult relationships:

> I always was really painfully shy, and I didn't date very much when I was in junior high school or high school. But I remember there were a few times when I actually asked a girl out and I would go out on a date, and invariably, just as I was about to leave the house, my mother would say something like: "Don't do anything that's going to bring me a package in nine months." It was intimating, "Don't get the girl pregnant." And here I was, barely able to ask for the date. The thought that I would

even end up kissing the girl on the first date was something, and I was being told not to do anything that would get a girl pregnant. I even remember being conscious that it was a ridiculous thing for her to say.

But somehow I think it really did affect me, because I remember when I was in college and started to have some relationships, the first time I attempted to be sexual with a woman was always particularly hard for me in terms of being able to come. Not even to get an erection, but just to finish the act of sexual intercourse. And I really think somewhere it inhibited my normal feeling of sexuality, just my normal feeling that I was okay and that I could feel sexual toward a woman without its being bad. And it was this little offhand remark that was meant to be funny—I don't think that I ever realized exactly what it did to me.

It is clear that many of the events we experienced during childhood and adolescence caused us to develop distorted ways of thinking about our bodies and our sexuality. These unhealthy attitudes have made sexuality an area that is often fraught with anxiety and pain. Although there has been some improvement recently, with people trying to talk more honestly about their sexuality, considerable damage remains.

Voices During Sex

The critical inner voice can be thought of as the spokesperson for the unhealthy point of view about sex. The voice influences people to deny themselves pleasure and causes them to give up their natural desires and wants and to conform to prohibitions learned early in childhood. Voice attacks related to sexuality are directed against our partners as well as ourselves. For example, a woman reported telling herself: *"Why should he* [her husband] *still be attracted to you? You're getting fat; you're not as young as you used to be."* She also had negative thoughts about her husband: *"He's not interested in sex anymore. He just falls asleep at night. When he is sexual it's so routine."* Both types of negative views (toward ourselves and our partners) can diminish our sexual feelings and cause us to hold back our affectionate and sexual responses.

Men and women experience many different types of voices during sex, criticizing their bodies, their sexual behavior, the way they move, and their own and their partner's level of excitement. These self-defeating thoughts can make us begin to think of sex as a performance to be judged, instead of its being a simple extension of affection and feelings of attraction.

Exercise 5.1: The Firestone Voice Scale for Sex

You can use exercise 5.1 to become familiar with negative thoughts that may be intruding into your sexual relating. If you like, make a copy of the questionnaire and ask your partner to fill it out.

Voices You May Be Aware of Before Making Love

Among the most common voices people have reported were self-protective warnings against becoming involved, both sexually and emotionally, with another person. Often when they feel like making a stronger commitment to the relationship, they experience critical inner voices warning them: *"Watch out! Don't get hooked on him (her). What if he (she) decides to break up after you've made love? Then you'll really feel terrible."*

You may be aware of certain voice attacks even before you are in a sexual situation. For example, since AIDS has become a serious concern, if you are considering starting a new sexual relationship, you may be telling yourself: *"What if he (she) is not telling you the truth about being tested for AIDS? What if he (she) has lower standards for safe sex than you do? How do you really know you can trust this person?"*

Men often worry about getting their partner pregnant and tell themselves: *"How do you know if she's really on the pill like she said? What if she's just trying to get pregnant? What makes you think she's trustworthy?"*

You may react in a negative way or feel like avoiding sex if your partner happens to be hesitant or less than enthusiastic. For example, Jim found that he felt awkward with his new girlfriend, as he put it, "when we were about to go from the living room into the bedroom." He reported that he found himself silently criticizing himself for taking the initiative: *"What makes you think she's interested in being with you? You're just forcing things, going too fast. You're so insensitive!"* After saying this voice, Jim continued: "Sometimes, these self-attacks are triggered if I think my girlfriend is being a little bit hesitant. I can't really tell which it is. I may already feel awkward and just not be seeing her right, or she may be self-conscious, too. But in any case, I begin to feel strange at that point, as though I'm mean to want to be sexual."

As people grow older, many tend to use their age as an excuse for limiting the frequency of their lovemaking. For example, they may tell themselves things like: *"People your age don't need that much sex. You should settle down and enjoy other things. After all, sex isn't the most important thing in your life now; you're so busy with your work, your friends. Sex is for young people, not for you."*

Many older men report hearing voices telling them: *"There's no fool like an old fool"* if they indicate a romantic or sexual interest in a woman. Sometimes older women tell themselves: *"You're too old and out of shape and wrinkled. Why would he still find you sexually attractive?"*

These voices are supported by common cliches casually repeated by other people and supported by attitudes in our society. One fifty-year-old woman was asked by her gynecologist during a routine examination: "How often do you still have sex?" For a number of weeks after that, she had negative thoughts attacking the frequency with which she and her husband made love. *"How much longer do you think you can keep this up? It's probably not good for you to be so sexually active at your age. It's kind of weird and abnormal, don't you think?"*

Critical Inner Voices You May Experience During Sex

During the sex act, many people experience negative thoughts that can have an adverse effect both on their feelings of excitement and on their sexual responses. At times, the intrusion of these thoughts can actually bring lovemaking to a standstill.

About Your Body

Self-depreciating thoughts about our physical appearance and our bodies often interfere with the flow of feelings during sex. For example, many women have self-conscious thoughts about their breasts such as: *"Your breasts are too small"*; *"They're too large, and not well-shaped"* or *"They look weird, you can't even wear a bathing suit because your breasts look so abnormal. So why would he want to touch your breasts?"* Or they have thoughts about their genital area: *"Your vagina is too large"* or *"It has an unpleasant odor. Don't let him touch you there. You might not be clean. Don't have oral sex, he'll be disgusted."*

By the same token, many men feel inadequate about the size of their penis, telling themselves: *"Your penis is too small. You won't be able to satisfy her. You're not going to last. You're not as manly as other men."* Interestingly, the areas of a person's body that are subject to the most criticism from the critical inner voice are the very ones that their partners often do not touch or caress. It seems that on a subliminal level, sexual partners are keyed into each other's critical inner voices.

About Your Sexual Performance

In the midst of making love, you may begin to experience negative thoughts about different aspects of your lovemaking, your level of excitement: *"You're not excited enough. You're not wet enough"* or *"You're not erect enough. You're not going to be able to have an orgasm."* Or you may have attacks on the way you are moving or your ability to please your partner: *"You're moving too much. He'll think you're a slut"* or *"You're hurting her. You're entering her too soon. She's not ready"* or *"You're not touching him or her right. You're not sensitive about what he (she) likes."* Often people have thoughts such as *"You just have to get through this somehow,"* and this focus on performance makes their lovemaking feel mechanical or impersonal.

Voices You May Experience After Making Love

Like many people, you may begin thinking back over your sexual experience. At this time, some people suffer a barrage of voices even when they felt good during the actual sex act. Paradoxically, people who have had an especially gratifying and emotionally meaningful sexual experience often have voice attacks predicting a negative experience in the future. These thoughts depreciate both partners and devalue their sexual experience. Some of the voices women typically have following a satisfying sexual experience include:

"So you felt really good? So what? You think you can feel like this all the time? Forget it! You'll probably be nervous and tense next time."

"You felt really good? So what! He didn't look so good afterward. It was probably a terrible experience for him. You probably scared him off by being so enthusiastic."

While many men reported telling themselves things like:

"She didn't look very happy afterwards. How do you know she had an orgasm? She might have faked it."

"You were lucky this time. Just wait, though, next time she'll find out how you really are sexually."

Identify the Critical Inner Voices That Interrupt a Sexual Experience

When our critical inner voice intrudes on our lovemaking, we often try to ignore it and become intent on simply completing the sex act. However, this solution usually leads to our feeling more distant emotionally from our partner. Instead, it is valuable to stop and talk about these thoughts—that is, to give them away to your partner without blame, as described in chapter 4. In this situation, it is important to maintain physical contact while revealing your critical inner voices. In other words, try not to allow your voice attacks to interfere with your physical embrace and closeness. As a result, your original feelings of excitement, attraction, and sexual desire may return, and you may continue making love. In any case, you will experience a resurgence of affectionate feelings and will be closer emotionally to your partner instead of feeling more distant.

For example, Ellen and George had been married a year when they began experiencing difficulties in their sexual relating. Earlier, the couple had learned in a workshop the technique of giving away their critical inner voices in a dialogue with each other. One evening, Ellen noticed that she had started to feel cut off from her feelings of excitement as the couple began to make love. She decided to apply what she had learned in the workshop and revealed to George how she was feeling. She said:

You know, I was feeling really excited and sexual with you, but then I started feeling scared. So I wanted to stop a minute and tell you some of the thoughts I was having. I started thinking: *"You're not feeling very much, what's the matter with you?"* Then I started thinking things about you. I know this sounds crazy, but I was questioning whether you really wanted to be with me. I know that I'm off in thinking this, but I wanted to give it away. Some of the critical voices I was hearing were: *"He doesn't want to be with you. You're not the person he wants to be with. You're not really that nice to him. He doesn't feel anything for you."* That last thought is so the opposite of how I believe you really feel that it's painful to even say it, it feels really uncomfortable to say it.

George told Ellen that he was glad that she suggested talking because he had been starting to feel cut off himself. He said:

> I wasn't feeling very much myself, and I started thinking: *"What's happened? She's fine, She seems excited. It must be you. You'd better make it okay again. You'd better fix it. Move a little faster: just try to finish it off, but don't let her know that there's something wrong with you, but don't make her think something is wrong with her, either."*

After Ellen and George disclosed their critical inner voices and shared their feelings, they felt very close to each other and resumed their lovemaking.

Exercise 5.2: What Your Critical Inner Voice Tells You About Sex

In exercise 5.2, on the left-hand side of the page, record the critical inner voices about sex that you have experienced. On the right-hand side, write what you really think about these voices.

How Do You Relate Sexually? Two Kinds of Sex

The way people relate sexually to their partners in terms of being emotionally close can vary considerably from one experience to the next. Just as there are two distinct ways of viewing sex, there are two different ways of relating sexually. These can be conceptualized as being two ends of a continuum. At one end is a healthy way of relating that involves genuine emotional contact and is a continuation of the affection, tenderness, and companionship between two people. At the other end is a style of sexual relating in which the partners are using sex simply to relieve tension or cut off feelings. This type of sexual experience can be a movement away from real intimacy and emotional exchange between two people and toward a reliance on sex as a mechanism for gratifying oneself in an inward style that limits true relating.

Sexual experiences appear to be the most fulfilling when they are an outgrowth of affectionate feelings. During lovemaking, whenever there is a switch from close emotional contact to a more self-gratifying style of relating, this transformation is hurtful to the well-being of both people. Many people report feelings of emptiness, a sense of dissatisfaction, and irritability after a sexual experience where a less personal kind of relating predominates.

The distinction between the two styles of sexual relating is not necessarily reflected by the stability, longevity, or depth of the relationship. Instead, what is significant is that each partner is aware of the other as a separate person instead of an instrument for his or her own gratification. Whenever sex is used for control, power play, manipulation, security, or self-soothing, it can be harmful for both partners.

There are several signs that can help alert us to the times when we may be cutting off from feeling close to our partners and are moving toward a more impersonal style of sexual relating: (1) holding back our sexual responses; (2) trying to control the sex act and our partner; (3) an overreliance on fantasy to increase excitement; and (4) the presence of negative thoughts prior to and during sexual intercourse, as described above.

Sexual Withholding

At times, we may find ourselves holding back or inhibiting our natural sexual desire and many of its expressions, such as physical affection and touching. As noted in chapter 3, many patterns of withholding are not conscious. When holding back sexual responses becomes habitual or long-lasting, it has a deadening effect on the feelings of excitement and attraction we would naturally experience.

Control

People who are sexually withholding often feel threatened by spontaneous sexual interactions and sexual intimacy. As a result, they may try to regulate or direct various aspects of the sex act—that is, they dictate the frequency of lovemaking, the time, the place, the conditions, movements, positions, and manner of expressing affection. Controlling these aspects of the sex act may diminish the fear they feel and make them feel safer. Most people experience these fear reactions on a level beneath their conscious awareness; they pull back before they are aware that they have become anxious or fearful.

Stephanie's marriage was a typical and unfortunate example of the consequences of sexual withholding and control. Because of her fears and insecurity, Stephanie began to hold back her affection and other positive responses soon after she was married. At the same time, she tried to control many aspects of the marriage. Her efforts to control were particularly evident in her sexual relationship.

Her husband, Ralph, who tended to seek definition from a woman, gradually submitted to her controlling manipulations and gave up his point of view. As a result of being withheld from, he became emotionally hungry and desperate for Stephanie's love and affection. As time went by, Ralph became more passive, desperate, and unattractive. In trying to please Stephanie and keep the relationship together, he surrendered his own wants. The couple eventually separated and later, in therapy, Stephanie tried to understand the factors that led to the dissolution of their marriage:

> When we were first married, the attacks started out toward my own sexuality, like: *"Don't get so excited. Don't be active. Don't move around so much."* But then the attacks ended up being on Ralph. It causes me a lot of pain because I know I supported the negative ways he felt about himself. Eventually I began to feel repelled by his touch. I had thoughts like:

"His touch doesn't feel good, it's too soft. He's just not a strong man; he's weak, so how could you feel that excited with him? Look, if you make love tonight, then you won't have to be sexual with him tomorrow. He's gotten used to that. You've done what's expected and you can relax. So just get it over with. Just let him feel enough to get it over with. Just lie there and don't move and let him do everything. He needs this. He needs it in order to feel good. Just give in to him and don't feel anything about it!"

I realize now how much I saw him as a weak person. I know now that I made him feel like that and that's when he became unattractive to me. And I felt terribly guilty, because I knew on some level that I had turned him into a person I couldn't love. I remember hating Ralph for letting me control him, even though it was something I worked at all the time.

When the therapist asked her why she was so insecure, Stephanie said:

Well, I felt like if I didn't control him, he wouldn't be there. I felt I wasn't likable enough to be chosen. I had to make sure he would always be there. This sounds so irrational, but I thought that if he were free enough even to choose which movie we went to, I was going to lose him. If he had that much freedom, he would never choose me.

You know, that's exactly how my mother was. And the relationship between my parents was like that. I didn't know there was any other way to live. I hated myself so much and felt so unlovable all the time that I was surprised that he had even chosen me in the first place. So I had to hold on to him.

Sexual Withholding, Control, and Sexual Abuse

In many cases, people who feel afraid or need to control the sexual situation, or who withhold sexual responses, have experienced sexual abuse as children. As adults, they often engage in promiscuous sexual behavior without becoming attached to anyone. When they do become involved in a more committed relationship, particularly one that combines emotional closeness and sexuality, they experience fear and react by either withholding their sexual responses or attempting to control various aspects of the sex act. They may not be consciously aware that they are afraid before they start to defend themselves. Memories of childhood sexual abuse often come to the surface in the challenging situation of a close, intimate sexual relationship.

For example, when Stephanie sought therapy to understand the causes of her failed marriage, she recalled incidents of inappropriate sexual behavior on the part of her father and also remembered sexual games that both parents had engaged in with her and her sisters. She recognized that her fears originated in a number of sexual abuses whose cumulative effects were to make her uncomfortable in intimate situations. Unconsciously, she had adopted the defenses of control and withholding to help her cope with her fear:

I was just thinking about all the feelings that I grew up with. I thought how I was treated in my family, particularly how my father acted toward me. And how he never was sweet toward me. He never showed me any affection in a nice way. It never was just that "you're a valuable child or a valuable girl." It was always for my looks, or what I could get for my looks. I know that had a large part to do with my insecurity. I never really learned to like myself just for myself. And that's why I could never believe that Ralph liked me for myself, because I never did.

Stephanie's memories were corroborated by her older sisters, who had experienced the same treatment. The oldest girls even reported having lured Stephanie and her youngest sister into participating in sexual games with them. These memories were painful for Stephanie to face, yet realizing what had happened to her helped her to develop compassion for herself and be less afraid of her sexual feelings as an adult.

How Fantasy Interferes with Intimacy

Many people put distance between themselves and their partner during sex by fantasizing. When we use fantasy as a way of increasing excitement, in a sense we are denying our need for our partner and retreating from being close emotionally. When there is a secretive element to this process, we feel guilty, especially when our sexual fantasies are about someone other than our partner.

Jerry, age fifty, spoke of his sexual relationship with his wife of ten years:

I'm most bothered these days by the loss of sexual excitement in my marriage. I feel excited before actually having sex and it makes me so look forward to making love. But then somehow I stop that excitement. It's ironic; the excitement and the relationship are available to me, but instead of feeling that, I substitute fantasies about having that same thing with somebody else.

Looking back over my marriage and even before I was married, I can see that this pattern has been operating for a long time. When I was dating, I would have that thrill and excitement with a woman until I developed a close relationship with her. Then the feelings would die and I would fantasize about someone new. It makes me sad to know that I've been missing a meaningful part of my life by creating fantasies about someone instead of being close to my wife, who is actually there for real and wanting to be close to me.

When I was a teenager my father told me that there were girls you had sex with and girls you didn't have sex with. Even though it was a humorous attempt at sex education on his part, I know it ties into this problem. I can't ever remember having a positive or sensitive talk with anyone about anything sexual. It was always "don't" or "be careful" or "here's who you do it with and who you don't." But there was never anything that indicated that there was a nice part to sex or that it was a mutual situation.

Exercise 5.3: An Imaginary Conversation About Your Sexuality

The exercise of carrying on a written dialogue about your sexuality with the parent you most identify with can be a powerful strategy for understanding the full scope of your critical inner voices and becoming more familiar with negative attitudes you have learned from your parents. In exercise 5.3, first write what the parent you most closely identify with would say about your sexuality, your partner, and your sexual relationship. Next, write what you would say back to him or her about these subjects. Composing these two points of view in this imagined dialogue can help you separate your own point of view from views held by your mother or father.

An Example of Exercise 5.3

The following is an excerpt from one woman's "imaginary conversation about your sexuality" exercise:

> What my mother would say about sex and men: You don't like sex. What's this stuff about being close during sex? It's not the time for all that bullshit! Sex is for men and it's all about what they get from it. What about their obsessions with women's breasts and hips? That's so disgusting—you see, it's all for them. Everything is so fascinating for them. *You're* the object for *their* desire. There's nothing fascinating about their bodies, so what's in it for you? Face it! Closeness and sex do *not* go together. Just say no! Don't show you're interested because you're not. And stay in control!

> What I would say back to my mother: You're wrong about everything. Just the thought of being close to my husband's body excites me. Men love to give women pleasure. It's a give-and-take situation. There is nothing like being sweet to him in bed. There is so much pleasure in touching, kissing, and caressing someone you love. Sex is about taking time to be intimate, close, soft, and in touch with your own sensations and body and mind. It's not about performing.

Moving Toward Increased Sexual Intimacy in Your Relationship

An exercise that has been helpful for increasing partners' tolerance for intimacy—the giving and accepting of physical affection—while maintaining emotional closeness, involves allowing each partner in turn to do whatever he or she wishes to do to the other. To begin this exercise, talk with your partner about any inhibitions or self-consciousness you might have in relation to expressing affection or accepting affection from him or her. Then, each of you in turn touches, strokes, massages, or sexually caresses the other. While you are engaged in this activity, it is recommended that you communicate the feelings and thoughts you are experiencing at the moment. The dialogue can include positive feelings as well as any negative voices you might be aware of while in the process of either giving or receiving affection. Do not feel surprised if you feel sad. The barriers we have erected to protect us from our sadness are the same barriers we are breaking down by being close and loving.

There are a wide range of distorted attitudes and thoughts that affect every phase of lovemaking. Using techniques and exercises derived from voice therapy to externalize these internal parental prescriptions can help you separate the angry, attacking part of yourself—the critical inner voice—from a more compassionate view—the real you. By becoming more aware of these thoughts and where they came from, you can free yourself from self-defeating, restrictive behaviors and significantly improve your sexual relationship.

Although many believe that the passion and sexual excitement they feel at the beginning of a relationship naturally fade because of familiarity, this does not have to happen. You can continue to experience sexual love and passion in your relationship beyond the early phases. By challenging the critical inner voices that intrude into your sexual relationship, both you and your partner will evolve and experience a kind of affection, companionship, and sexuality that is uniquely satisfying.

Exercise 5.1: Firestone Voice Scale for Sex

Circle the frequency with which you experience the following critical inner voices:

0 = Never   1 = Rarely   2 = Once in a while   3 = Frequently   4 = Most of the time

0 1 2 3 4   Sex has always been a problem. Why bother with it? There are more important things in life.

0 1 2 3 4   He (she) always has an excuse for not wanting to make love.

0 1 2 3 4   You'd better keep an eye on him (her). He (she) might cheat.

0 1 2 3 4   The next time he'll (she'll) find out what you're really like.

0 1 2 3 4   Your breasts are too small/large.

0 1 2 3 4   Your penis is too small.

0 1 2 3 4   Sex is for young people. You're too old for sex.

0 1 2 3 4   You might get pregnant. (You might get her pregnant.)

0 1 2 3 4   How do you know he (she) is telling you the truth about being tested for AIDS?

0 1 2 3 4   You always give in. You have no standards.

0 1 2 3 4   He's (she's) so cold and unresponsive.

0 1 2 3 4   He (she) is probably cheating on you right now!

0 1 2 3 4   He (she) probably says the same things to all the men (women) he (she) dates.

0 1 2 3 4   He (she) doesn't know how to touch you.

0 1 2 3 4   How do you know she had an orgasm? It was probably a bad experience for her.

0 1 2 3 4   All men are interested in is sex. They don't like emotional commitments.

0 1 2 3 4   You're not erect enough. You won't be able to satisfy her.

0 1 2 3 4   He (she) will never call you again. It was a terrible experience for him (her).

0 1 2 3 4   He (she) doesn't care about your sexual needs.

0 1 2 3 4   Women are tricky about sex. They're just trying to trap you into marriage.

Exercise 5.2: What Your Critical Inner Voice Tells You About Sex

My critical inner voice

Before sex

_____

_____

_____

_____

During sex

_____

_____

_____

_____

After sex

_____

_____

_____

_____

My realistic thoughts

Before sex

_____

_____

_____

_____

During sex

_____

_____

_____

_____

After sex

_____

_____

_____

_____

Exercise 5.3: An Imaginary Conversation About Your Sexuality

What would your mother/father say about your sexuality, your partner, and your sexual relationship?

What would my mother/father say?

_____

_____

_____

_____

_____

_____

_____

_____

What would I say back to my mother/father?

_____

_____

_____

_____

_____

_____

_____

_____

Chapter 6

How the Critical Inner Voice Seduces You into Addictive Behaviors

The voices . . . are very real. . . . These voices exist to reign over the victim's mind; every action and thought is based on the direction given by this commanding presence.

—Marcia D., "Abandoned Beliefs: Anorexia's Voices" (Web site)

In this chapter, we describe behaviors that not only limit people's ability to pursue their goals in life, but that can also be detrimental to their physical health and emotional well-being. These addictive patterns may not be immediately life-threatening, but they do diminish the quality of our lives, and they are so widespread in our society that they are often considered normal. What all of these behaviors have in common is that they help us cut off painful feelings, and that they are influenced by the critical inner voice. Therefore, it is important to identify the destructive thoughts that govern these behaviors and challenge them by finding better ways to cope with painful situations and the stresses that invariably arise in everyday life.

How Addictive Behaviors Affect You

When we use the strategy of suppressing our feelings to avoid emotional pain and anxiety, we end up not only blocking out pain but limiting our emotions of joy and exhilaration as well. When many of us were children, the defenses or methods that we used to relieve our pain became addictive because, like drugs, they temporarily made us feel better. But as with the drug addict, we become less able to cope with life and more and more limited by the effects of cutting off from our feelings. When we suppress our feelings, we tend to become disengaged from ourselves and, as a result, have difficulty developing a real sense of ourselves.

Whenever these suppressed feelings threaten to break through to conscious awareness, we begin to feel anxious. This can lead to a destructive cycle, because then we feel that we must do something more to cut off our anxiety. We usually turn to another familiar, yet self-defeating method of coping. In fact, living a defended life is similar to having a serious addiction, because it consumes our energy and resources. On the other hand, when we choose a life that is vulnerable and open, in which we feel both the joy and the pain of living, a good deal of our natural energy is liberated.

It is often difficult for people who have experienced considerable pain early in life to give up the negative views, behaviors, and activities that they adopted as coping mechanisms. Nevertheless, maintaining cynical attitudes, addictive habit patterns, and self-defeating behaviors is more damaging in the long run than taking chances and even being hurt again.

A lifestyle that cuts off feelings is characterized by an overreliance on self-nurturing habits, rituals, and routines. It is based on the illusion that a person is self-sufficient. This sense of false independence—the fantasy bond—contrasts with a life of real independence, which necessarily involves real exchanges with real people in a real world.

In this chapter, we describe behaviors as well as activities that can become addictive, focus on methods for challenging the critical inner voices that support them, and provide suggestions for better ways to cope with painful feelings in life. First, we turn our attention to events in our childhoods and investigate how we learned these ways of soothing ourselves.

How Do We Come to Develop Addictions?

How do people become addicted to certain substances, objects, or activities? Where does the process of addiction begin? First, it is important to understand that fantasy and addiction are closely related. Human beings have the remarkable capacity to imagine, yet this ability can be both a strength and a weakness.

If we were physically or emotionally deprived as children, we learned to use fantasy to fill the void and to partly gratify our basic needs and relieve our pain. We developed the fantasy bond, a style of self-parenting or taking care of ourselves that can be thought of as a closed system in which we are both parent and child.

The parental part of this self-parenting system has two functions: it is soothing and nourishing as well as punishing and depreciating to the child part. Very early in life, we begin to use self-soothing behaviors such as thumb-sucking or rubbing a blanket to try to relieve our frustration and emotional pain. These methods partly work, and therefore they support our fantasy that we can take care of ourselves, that we don't need anything from the outside world. Later, we develop more elaborate self-soothing behaviors such as nail-biting, masturbation, TV watching, and reading to numb ourselves. These habits eventually become addictive because they help us manage anxiety or pain.

As adults, we often numb ourselves more directly with food, alcohol, and various drugs, or we become intensely involved in habitual routines, rituals, and activities that reduce our tension. The more we were emotionally deprived and frustrated as children, the more we will tend to rely on addictive defenses that increasingly incapacitate us, yet give us an illusion of self-sufficiency.

For example, as an infant, Edward was extremely agitated, and was labeled by his parents as "high-strung and temperamental." In spite of being knowledgeable about children (his mother was a teacher and his father a psychologist), his parents tried to relieve his symptoms by offering him whatever would immediately placate him. His mother reported that "from the very first day, Edward was extremely tense, hyperactive, and agitated until I put a pacifier in his mouth. Then his body would relax completely and he would actually breathe a loud sigh of relief."

Edward was the last of three sons born close together. At the time of his birth, his mother was preoccupied with her career and withdrawn from her husband. She was uncomfortable with Edward's crying and did not want him to disturb her schedule or her routines. Edward's father was cut off from his feelings to a certain extent and tried to make up for his wife's neglect of their three children by indulging them.

As the boy grew older, his parents continued to provide him with more sophisticated ways of soothing his pain, including a television for his bedroom, a stereo, and video games; when he was nine, they bought him a computer of his own. Edward developed a pattern of isolating himself in his room. His parents seemed to be happy as long as he was not bothering them. Edward rarely played with other children or took part in any school activities. His only interests were music and designing computer programs. At the age of twelve, he began to take drugs, beginning with marijuana and progressing to crack, and supported his habit through minor thefts. As an adult, Edward lived at home in a small guest house in the backyard until he was twenty-three. His parents seemed oblivious to his drug habit. Later, he was fired from his first job because of incompetency brought about by his excessive drug use. When Edward finally entered a rehabilitation program, his mother told the counselors, "Edward was addicted from birth."

It is clear that Edward's early environment contributed to his adopting a life of addiction. First, his agitation and frequent crying were misperceived by his parents as being an inherent part of his temperament. As a result, they failed to address the underlying factors that may have been causing his early distress. Instead, their focus was on quieting his crying, which was disturbing their lives. Second, the ongoing emotional deprivation he suffered, together with his parents' overindulgence and indifference to his real needs, crystallized Edward's tendency to cut off his pain through addictive behaviors. In a sense, they inadvertently trained him to be an addict.

How the Critical Inner Voice Encourages Addictive Behaviors

People who have an eating disorder, who indulge in drug or alcohol abuse, or who work to the point of exhaustion are all acting out self-destructive tendencies promoted by the critical inner voice. These habit patterns are direct assaults against our physical health and emotional well-being, and often lead to a gradual deterioration in our ability to function effectively in life.

The critical inner voice that controls addictive behavior takes two contradictory forms. First it encourages us to engage in the behavior: *"You've done great on your diet. What's the harm in having one small piece of cake?"* or *"You've had a rough week. You deserve a drink"* or *"Johnny is going to have other Little League games. You can work late tonight, it won't matter."* We then often act according to the suggestions of the voice and overeat, drink too much, or work too hard.

At this point, the destructive thoughts switch in their tone and become extremely punishing, which makes it clear that the voice is not a conscience or a moral guide—it plays both sides of the coin. The voice ruthlessly criticizes us for having engaged in the very behavior it had encouraged: *"You weak-willed jerk, you said you were going to stay on your diet. You never stick to anything"*; *"You creep, you said you weren't going to drink anymore, and there you go, drinking again"*; *"You're such a negligent father! You told Johnny you'd be at the game!"*

After a barrage of self-attacks, we feel worse and experience a great deal of emotional pain, turmoil, and distress. In this state, the critical voice is more likely to influence us to again engage in the addictive behavior to numb our pain, ease our agitation, or get rid of the feeling, which completes the cycle: *"You've gone off your diet already. What difference will it make if you eat the rest of the cake?"*; *"Go on, have another drink."*

Listening to this type of punishing voice makes us feel worse; it is obvious that it would not inspire us to try to change our behavior in a positive direction. Hating ourselves for a behavior and running ourselves down never leads to behavior change. We even feel justified in our self-attacks because we have the goods on ourselves; however, this process is merely one part of a destructive cycle.

These critical inner voices appear to be an imitation of the ways our parents defended or numbed themselves. In other words, if your father drank when he felt stressed, you are more likely to take on this behavior. Or if your mother over-ate to get rid of anxiety, you are likely to adopt this pattern without even thinking about it.

Eating Disorders, Drug Abuse, and Alcoholism

The critical inner voice plays a major role in eating disorders, drug abuse, and alcoholism, first seducing the person, then punishing him or her for indulging. It is difficult to break these patterns, because the anxiety that has been relieved by the use of these substances resurfaces during withdrawal. Powerful emotions of sadness or rage often emerge when people attempt to abstain from their excessive use of drugs or alcohol.

For example, Kay, twenty-five, had abused drugs since her early teens. She remembered that when she was around twelve, she began to feel different from her peers and alienated from them:

> I felt so angry and often acted defiantly at school. Sometimes I even threw a temper tantrum. Then my friends introduced me to marijuana. It was a perfect setup. It took the edge off all those feelings, the pain and the anger. I was more social when I felt high and mellow. I became almost completely addicted to this "perfect"' method for getting rid of my feelings. Every attempt that my parents made to get me off drugs met with failure because I immediately started up again.
>
> I really learned how to suppress those feelings. Whenever the drug I was currently using stopped having much effect, I moved on to something else. I spent the next fifteen years always dependent on a drug. When each would stop working for me, I would move on to stronger and stronger drugs. I was never able to form close relationships or a stable work situation. The drug always came first. Pain would start to come up any time I would have a feeling of being a failure, of not living up to my parents' expectations, and I would stop the pain with more drugs.
>
> There would be times when I tried to kick drugs, but then there would be the voices urging me to take drugs again: *"You really need to take the edge off." "This job is so boring, so physically painful, you need to do something to get rid of the pain."* Then after I indulged, I would have thoughts like, *"You are a total failure!" "You never stick to anything you decide." "You are never going to amount to anything."* And I would feel worse and worse and turn back to drugs to relieve the pain. Finally, I was injured in a car accident, which was the perfect excuse to start

taking Vicodin. Then when the doctor took me off Vicodin, I realized I had a serious problem.

At this point, Kay sought psychotherapy and learned how to identify the critical inner voices that had influenced her to use drugs. Her therapist first encouraged Kay to write a personal history that included a description of important events in her childhood, her current relationships, her personal and vocational concerns, and her aspirations and goals in life. Writing this history helped Kay develop an overall picture of her present situation and the circumstances in her childhood that may have contributed to her need to numb herself with drugs.

Next, Kay and her therapist developed a plan to counter her destructive thoughts by gradually decreasing the frequency of her drug use. She would now be going against the prescriptions of the voice by refusing to succumb to its seductive prodding. This regimen was put into place after Kay consulted with her physician about the side effects of withdrawal.

Kay's therapist suggested that Kay become aware of specific times when she started to experience thoughts urging her to take drugs. She was to record in a daily journal the situations and experiences that triggered her craving for relief, as well as events that contributed to her painful mood swings or that made her feel upset. The therapist told her that it was important for her to recognize the critical inner voices as they occurred; however, it was not necessary for her to either agree or disagree with them. She simply needed to recognize that she was beginning to attack herself.

Kay was encouraged to pay particular attention to the seductive nature of these destructive thoughts, rather than surrendering to their goading or accepting their self-depreciating statements as an accurate evaluation of her. She discovered that merely acknowledging that she was involved in a process of self-attack was often effective in making the troublesome thoughts recede into the background. In addition, simply recognizing that she was attacking herself had the effect of decreasing the influence that the critical inner voice had been exerting on her overall mood.

To strengthen her real self, Kay began to initiate behaviors that were more consistent with her personal and vocational goals. She made efforts to become increasingly assertive at work and began to engage in activities that had interested her during periods when she had not been dependent on drugs. In collaboration with her therapist, Kay reviewed the personal history she had written at the onset of therapy and focused on the wants, aspirations, and goals, both personal and vocational, that she had described there.

While keeping the daily journal, Kay noticed that the feelings of anxiety and emotional pain that emerged as she decreased her drug use made her feel bad or down at times. However, she made a conscious decision to behave "as if" the feelings were not as painful as she experienced them. She was determined to continue functioning in her job "as if" she were competent and capable instead of incompetent and weak. She found that this strategy worked, because her feelings gradually caught up with the way she was acting. In other words, she began to feel more self-confident and relaxed *after* she had made a concerted effort to behave as though she were okay during work hours. Later, Kay generalized this strategy to other areas of her life with the same positive results.

There are several steps that Kay went through as she gave up her long-standing addiction to drugs. First, she recognized that she was rationalizing her use of prescription drugs by believing she needed to medicate herself because of her recent injury. This insight convinced her to seek treatment, where she learned the methods of challenging the critical inner voice. Second, she began to uncover the critical inner voices that had played such a decisive role in her maintaining her drug habit. Third, she adopted various strategies to strengthen her sense of self and moved toward pursuing her goals in life once again. At the same time that she was seeking more constructive ways of coping with painful aspects of living, she was reaffirming her commitment to pursue the wants and goals she had described in her personal history.

How Compulsive Activities Can Become Addictive

There are countless rituals and activities that people engage in to numb feelings of pain and distress. Routines or rituals that temporarily reduce our anxiety have the potential to become habitual or addictive. It is important to emphasize that many originally healthy or neutral activities can eventually come to fill an addictive function if they are done compulsively and if they are used to help us avoid feelings or relieve tension or anxiety. When we perform a certain routine over and over, we often become dulled to painful feelings because the repetition of an activity gives us a sense of certainty and permanence in a life that is filled with uncertainty and impermanence.

Anyone can become "addicted" to or compulsive about any activity when it is carried to an extreme. Many of these activities may be considered acceptable or even desirable, such as working hard, exercising, browsing the Internet, and shopping. These kinds of activities are potentially addictive because they are usually done in isolation, and they act to cut off your feelings, leaving you numb or dulled.

When a behavior or ritual becomes a compulsion, we need to continuously repeat the behavior so that the feelings we have suppressed will not reemerge. For example, many children as well as adults sit glued to their television sets day after day, while others spend hours playing video games, to the detriment of important activities in their lives, and to the exclusion of personal contact with friends and family members.

In the following excerpts, an adult son and daughter write about their father's compulsive style of working and how it affected them.

Son's Journal

It seems that when my father was really young, he had been robbed of the ability to feel the satisfaction of real accomplishment. He worked constantly, as if my grandfather were still critically supervising his labor. As each household project was completed to perfection, he would move on to the next without looking at or feeling anything about the final product.

He'd come home from work about 7 P.M., and march into the backyard without changing his clothes, so that soon all his fine suits had tattered knees and splashes of paint. He'd work endlessly into the night until the neighbors would call and ask him to please quit sawing or to turn off his work lights so their children could sleep. He'd work in downpours and in the blazing sun for hours as if he were immune to the elements and his own fatigue. He worked as if his problems would cease with the completion of each project, but of course they didn't.

Daughter's Journal

I know that the way my father worked all the time really affected me. I feel like I'm good only if I'm really driving myself at work. I get really scared if I'm not working all the time. It seems so irrational, but in my day-to-day life, if I start to think more about love, about my husband, about people I care about, about my children, I get really scared and I run back to the other way of being, working long hours and exhausting myself. It's a much more comfortable way for me to live, to allow myself to have just little pieces of affection, just brief times to be with my husband and children. I have to balance my life in the other direction, though, where I'm good and I'm working hard and I'm driven.

Guidelines for Challenging Addictive Behaviors

There are several exercises that are useful for identifying the specific critical inner voices that may be contributing to your addictive behavior. It is important to remember that the inner voices that encourage an addictive behavior or lessen any resolve you may have about not engaging in the behavior sound positive and kindly toward you, yet they are directing you to act against your goals and priorities.

Identify Critical Inner Voices That First Seduce and Then Punish You

As in the case of Kay, recognizing that you may be using substances in a way that is harmful to you is the first step in breaking your dependency on them. Identifying the voices that urge you to engage in an addictive behavior is the next step in challenging and going against them.

Exercise 6.1: The Firestone Voice Scale for Addictions

Exercise 6.1 can be helpful in strengthening your resolution to gradually give up a behavior that has been detrimental to your physical health and emotional well-being. Identifying both the negative attitudes toward yourself and the seemingly positive inner voices that are trying to seduce you into engaging in an addictive behavior will make it easier for you to eventually gain control over the behavior.

Seductive and Punishing Thoughts and Feelings That Accompany Addictive Behavior

In battling an addiction, it is important that you become aware of the times when you feel the most tempted to indulge in an addictive habit pattern. At these times, turn your focus to the feelings of anxiety, anger, or sadness that emerge when you refuse to give in to temptation.

If you decide to stop smoking, for example, you could keep a daily journal of the thoughts and feelings that arise when you feel like having a cigarette. What does the critical inner voice say when you don't give in and have one? How does this leave you feeling? When people record their emotional reactions at the specific times when the temptation to indulge is overwhelming, they are better able to maintain their resolution to abstain. If they keep abstaining, these negative thoughts eventually recede and no longer have power over them.

Exercise 6.2: Voices of Addiction: Feelings and the Real You

In exercise 6.2, on the left-hand side of the page, record the inner voices that are seducing you to indulge and the voices that are then punishing you for indulging. In the middle column, record the feelings that these different voices arouse in you. In the right-hand column, write your realistic point of view. (Use more paper if you need to.)

Identify Triggering Events

Recovering substance abusers have found that it is vital to identify their *triggers*; that is, the specific cues in the environment that increase their urge to use. For example, many drug users feel the pull to use drugs when they are with peers who also use, or when there is empty time that leaves them feeling alone with their feelings. At these times, negative thoughts usually emerge. For this reason, it is important to think about the events or situations in your everyday life when you feel the most tempted to use your drug of choice.

Exercise 6.3: Triggers for Using Substances

This exercise is provided to help you identify the events that trigger you to abuse substances. On the left-hand side of the page, write down the situations, social interactions, or experiences that trigger the critical inner voices of addiction. In the middle column, record what your critical inner voice is saying at these times. On the right-hand side of the page, write down your realistic point of view. (Use more paper if you need to.)

Strengthen Your Real Self

The critical inner voice is "an overlay on the personality" (Firestone 1988). Just as the voice conceals our real self, addictions cover over and keep our real feelings at bay. As we give up behaviors dictated by the critical inner voice, our real self—the core of our personality—increasingly emerges and takes precedence over the enemy within. As noted earlier, our real self is made up of our wants, desires, and special goals. As we give up our addictive behaviors and begin to regain the multitude of feelings we have been suppressing for years, we become more aware of the wants and desires that are a fundamental part of our unique identity.

However, many people believe on a deep level that they cannot face the painful feelings they cut off from during childhood. Therefore, we are often reluctant to give up the self-soothing behaviors that have been keeping these feelings submerged. Sometimes it may seem easier to gratify ourselves with food, drugs, or habitual activities rather than to go through the intense longing and wanting we experienced as children, when our needs were not met. It may feel as though we are as vulnerable and helpless as we were at that time, when we were totally dependent on our parents to keep us alive. This is a feeling that almost everyone has as they give up an addiction and experience the emotions they have long suppressed. Until we have gone through an experience in our adult lives where we are able to honestly face our frustrations, we can never know that the present situation is different from our childhood. We need to learn, on an emotional level, that we can no longer be hurt to the same degree as we could be when we were children.

To become more aware of the reasons why you may be afraid to pursue your real goals in your life and in your personal relationships, it may be worthwhile to write a personal history, as Kay did—that is, (1) to describe the events in your childhood that you think may have influenced you to turn to self-soothing mechanisms, and (2) to identify the activities you enjoy, your special interests, and your wants and aspirations.

Writing a narrative about your life can be helpful in a number of ways. First, by recording early painful experiences of deprivation, you may become more aware of why these experiences made it necessary for you to cut off your feelings and why you had to learn to cope with life by using fantasy and addictive behaviors. Second, writing your personal history can help you make a sharp distinction between the past and the present. As a result, you will be able to challenge the belief that you cannot survive if you have to face again the painful longings and the rejection you experienced early in life. Generally speaking, recognizing that things are different in your life today can help you challenge your fear of taking a chance again on seeking satisfaction in real goals and real relationships.

Third, the information you write down in your personal history will make you more aware of your special wants, priorities, and goals. This awareness is vital as you begin to uncover your unique point of view about your relationships and your life, and as you move toward your stated goals. Gradually, each of these steps will enhance your real self while diminishing the power of your critical inner voice.

Learn to Pursue What You Want in Life

As you give up an addictive behavior, it is important to pursue what you want in your adult life. One way to go about this is to set definite goals for what you want to accomplish in your career and in your relationships (as described in exercises 3.1 and 4.5).

First, record these goals in your journal and then write down the actions you need to take in order to accomplish them. Keep track of each time you participate in the activities, projects, or friendships that are special to you. At first, you may not feel much like taking on a new project or activity. However, you can choose to act "as if" you are energetic and assertive, as Kay did in the example in this chapter. You may find that your feelings eventually catch up with your actions.

As you move in the direction of achieving your goals, you will come to recognize that what you want as an adult is very different from what you needed as a child. As you give up an addiction or self-soothing routine, you realize that you can never obtain the gratification or the kind of love that you needed so desperately as a child. However, these needs are no longer vital to your survival or happiness as an adult.

Exercise 6.4: Going After What You Want

In this exercise, list the wants, goals, and interests that are particularly important to you personally on the left-hand side of the page. In the middle column, list any critical inner voices that might prevent you from asking for what you want. On the right-hand side of the page, write a realistic point of view about your wants.

As you give up destructive behaviors that have been a part of your life for years, you may feel disoriented at times and may experience renewed voice attacks. These reactions will gradually subside if you decide to "sweat through" these periods of anxiety and temporarily increased self-attacks. As you give up your dependence on drugs or alcohol or other addictions, you will probably find that you have more energy to devote to your relationships.

We live in a largely addictive society that continues to reinforce the defenses that we learned as children; this reinforcement comes in the form of a negative social pressure to soothe ourselves, to try to obtain instant gratification. Soothing oneself appears to be an accepted way of life in our culture. Today many people who suffered deprivation in childhood continue to accept substitute gratifications in the form of drugs, alcohol, tobacco, television, video games, overwork, and other activities that distract them from experiencing their real lives.

Most people suffer from some degree of addiction that interferes with their living fully. We can successfully challenge these addictions if we come to terms with the painful feelings and frustrations that have caused us to cut off our feelings through the use of substances, routines, and activities.

Giving up an addiction or an activity that has become compulsive means that you will be taking a chance; it means removing your protective armor while still wondering if there is danger. If you are willing to take that chance and sweat through the anxiety and fear aroused when you give up your defended posture, you will find that you are living with dignity, sensitivity, and self-respect and, at the same time, coping more effectively with the pressures of everyday life.

When we have the courage to give up an addictive behavior or tension-reducing routine, we recover the feelings that we cut ourselves off from early in our lives. When we break through our armor of defenses, we reach the sadness and the vitality of our real selves, enabling us to live in a world in which our experiences are open-ended, instead of continually reliving our past.

If you are seriously involved in using drugs, alcohol, or other substances to soothe your pain and anxiety, it may be important that you seek professional help or join a group specifically devoted to helping people who are recovering from substance abuse.

Exercise 6.1: The Firestone Voice Scale for Addictions

Circle the frequency with which you experience the following critical inner voices:

0 = Never   1 = Rarely   2 = Once in a while   3 = Frequently   4 = Most of the time

0 1 2 3 4   You need a drink (hit, pill) so you can relax.

0 1 2 3 4   You went off your diet again! You have no willpower.

0 1 2 3 4   You've had a hard day. Take the edge off.

0 1 2 3 4   You're so angry; take something, mellow out.

0 1 2 3 4   Look at all the trouble you're causing your family by going back on your resolution to give up alcohol (drugs).

0 1 2 3 4   Have another cookie (drink, hit). What harm can it do?

0 1 2 3 4   It's okay for you to get high. You know how to maintain.

0 1 2 3 4   You've had a hard week. You need to relax. Have a drink (hit).

0 1 2 3 4   You used again. You're hopeless!

0 1 2 3 4   You've already blown your diet, so you might as well have whatever you want.

0 1 2 3 4   You're probably one of those people who has a metabolism problem, so why should you try to control your weight?

0 1 2 3 4   Just look at yourself in the mirror! You're so fat. You should get rid of that big meal you just ate.

0 1 2 3 4   You can easily control your weight by throwing up.

0 1 2 3 4   They can tell that you ate, that you are a disgusting pig.

0 1 2 3 4   What are you going to do with all this free time? You need something to fill the time and make you relax.

0 1 2 3 4   You can eat anything you want and get rid of it later.

0 1 2 3 4   You ate too much; you've got to purge.

0 1 2 3 4   You're a fat pig!

0 1 2 3 4   You don't deserve to eat anything.

0 1 2 3 4   If you want to feel good, then don't eat.

0 1 2 3 4   People want you to be fat.

0 1 2 3 4   Food is your worst enemy.

0 1 2 3 4   You'll gain weight if you take even one bite.

Exercise 6.2: Voices of Addiction: Feelings and the Real You

My critical inner voices	How these voices make me feel	My realistic thoughts

Seductive voices:

_____   _____   _____

_____   _____   _____

_____   _____   _____

_____   _____   _____

_____   _____   _____

_____   _____   _____

_____   _____   _____

Punishing voices:

_____   _____   _____

_____   _____   _____

_____   _____   _____

_____   _____   _____

_____   _____   _____

_____   _____   _____

Exercise 6.3: Triggers for Using Substances

Triggering events or circumstances	My critical inner voices	My realistic point of view

Exercise 6.4: Going After What You Want

Personal wants and desires	My critical inner voices	My realistic point of view

Chapter 7

How Listening to Your Critical Inner Voice Can Make You Feel Down and Depressed

I could not sleep, although tired, and lay feeling my nerves shaved to pain and the groaning inner voice: oh, you can't teach, can't do anything. Can't write, can't think ... I have a good self, that loves skies, hills, ideas, tasty meals, bright colors. My demon would murder this self by demanding that it be a paragon, and saying it should run away if it is anything less.

—Sylvia Plath

Depression strikes approximately one out of every five Americans. When people become depressed, their mood and feelings are disturbed and their perceptions of themselves, other people, and the world are distorted. Seriously depressed individuals tend to be persistently sad or anxious, feel restless or irritable, and experience a loss of interest or pleasure in the activities they once enjoyed.

Depression ranges from mild to moderate to very serious; it can be thought of as existing on a continuum in terms of the extent to which the depressed person actually believes or accepts the distortions of himself or herself, of others, and of the world promoted by the critical inner voice.

Depression is also directly related to the frequency with which a person experiences critical inner voices, and to the intensity of those voices. Moderately to seriously depressed people have reached a stage where the balance shifts in such a way that the negative point of view of the voice becomes dominant in their personality. For whatever reason, whether because of overwhelming frustration, a deep sense of loss, or even a positive event beyond their level of tolerance, they are now more against themselves than for themselves. Their distorted beliefs appear to them to be true representations of reality, even though they appear to be inaccurate or highly unlikely to other people. In other words, people who have become seriously depressed have come to believe the negative hostile statements of the critical inner voice about themselves and others.

In his book *Transforming the Mind* (2000), His Holiness the Fourteenth Dalai Lama addresses the issue of how the critical inner voice contributes to a depressed mood:

> Why is it that we don't succeed in enjoying the lasting happiness that we are seeking? And why are we so often faced with suffering and misery instead? . . . Since we lack the mental discipline needed to tame [our thoughts and emotions] . . . they control us. And thoughts and emotions, in their turn, tend to be controlled by our negative impulses rather than our positive ones. We need to reverse this cycle, so that our thoughts and emotions are freed from their subservience to negative impulses, and so we ourselves, as individuals, gain control of our own minds.

In this chapter, suggestions are provided that can help you free yourself from "negative impulses"—that is, from the thoughts and feelings generated by the critical inner voice that cause you to feel down or depressed. It is important to recognize that as intelligent and knowledgeable as you are, your critical inner voice has all of that intelligence and knowledge at its disposal to use for its own ends, which are to undermine your positive feelings about yourself and your life.

This does not mean that life isn't filled with situations and events that would make anyone feel bad, angry, sad, or anxious. Indeed, there are innumerable events that occur during our lifetimes that cause us real grief, sadness, and anxiety: the death of a loved one or close friend; loss of a job or income; a seemingly impossible work situation; rejection by a close friend, lover, or mate; a physical illness or disability. In fact, simply viewing scenes on the evening news depicting tragic events that occur each day throughout the world is enough to make us feel cynical, disillusioned, and momentarily depressed. Although these events and other hardships in life often make us feel upset and discouraged, it is the way we think about these events or situations that determines both the immediate and ongoing effect they will have on us.

As we emphasized in chapter 1, critical inner voices reside within our own minds, and if we consistently listen to and believe them, they greatly influence our perspective on life, including whether or not it is worth living. Negative events act as triggering mechanisms that can set off a downward spiral of thoughts, making us turn against ourselves and arousing the kinds of painful emotions that torment seriously depressed individuals. What starts this negative spiral is the way we react to or interpret those events. The way we explain such a situation or incident to ourselves is far more important than the event itself in influencing our mood.

Have You Ever Been Depressed?

You may experience depression as a temporary mood; you just feel down or discouraged for a short time. This is a state of mind that almost everyone gets into occasionally. Or you may be more seriously depressed, experiencing deep psychological pain and suffering for longer periods of time. If you are mildly depressed, you can see the light at the end of the tunnel, and you know you will feel better sooner or later. However, if you are experiencing a more serious depression, you cannot tell where the end of the tunnel is (or believe it has one), much less see any light, and you may need professional help before you can feel better. To understand depression, it is important that you become familiar with how the critical inner voice interprets unfortunate events in your life in ways that can lead to a depressed mood.

How Do You Usually React to Negative Events in Your Life?

Have you noticed that whenever you have one negative thought, it is nearly always followed by others? The stream of negative thoughts that follows a negative event can take on its own momentum. If left unchallenged, the thoughts, attacks, and worries escalate and expand into a nagging running commentary that can make you feel terrible about almost everything in your life. People tend to extend their negative thoughts about one particular situation to many other situations and end up feeling gloomy and down in their overall outlook.

To identify some of the important life events that can trigger negative thoughts in you, first think back to a time when you felt the worst you ever have. Try to recall the event that affected you then—it may have been a rejection, a move, or any incident that held significant meaning for you, including the loss of a loved one. Do you remember what you thought when this event occurred? What were you telling yourself about the event—what it meant about you and your life? Do you recall the emotions you experienced? How long were you upset or sad? Try to determine if the negative thoughts about this event spilled over into a general feeling about your life. For example, did you feel that in some way what had happened was your fault? Afterward, did you start feeling that almost everything was your fault?

Exercise 7.1: Depression and Life Events: Your Critical Inner Voice/The Real You

After you have considered these questions and your answers, you may find it worthwhile to use exercise 7.1 to explore the train of thoughts and core beliefs that were reinforced by your interpretation of this event. Were there other events that became associated with this one in your mind? Did this event and your reactions contribute to an overall belief that you still hold?

In exercise 7.1, the first step is to identify a period in your life when you felt the absolute worst you've ever felt. On the left-hand side of the page, describe the event or situation that you think triggered the terrible feelings at that time. Next, try to remember any critical inner voices that you experienced during or after the event and record these thoughts in the middle column. On the right-hand side of the page, write a realistic evaluation of the triggering event as you see it now. Is there a pattern you can identify in which similar events in your life have triggered these critical inner voices? Are you able now to give a realistic appraisal of the triggering event and your role in it? If not, you may still be believing your critical inner voice's point of view, and you may be experiencing depression.

An Example of Exercise 7.1

Here is an excerpt from the journal of a woman named Arlene:

Triggering event	Critical inner voices I recall experiencing at the time of the event	My realistic thoughts about the event *now*
When I was 12, my mother died after a long illness. I had helped take care of her while she was sick. Her last "order" to me, as she was carried out to an ambulance to go to the hospital, was to take care of my little brother, who was 9 at the time.	*"It's your fault she's dead. You didn't take good care of her. So what makes you think you can take care of your brother? He won't listen to you, won't obey you. You'll never live up to your mother's last wish."*	Of course, it's not my fault that she's dead. That's ridiculous! And it was so unrealistic of her to think I could take total care of my brother when I was only 12.

What Does It Feel Like to Be Depressed?

You can see how the kinds of critical thoughts that Arlene experienced would arouse very powerful feelings. Her self-attacks disrupted her normal grieving process, leaving her with unresolved feelings of loss that significantly affected her as an adult.

In addition to identifying the critical inner voices that are triggered by a tragic event or distressing situation, it is important that we become aware of the feelings that are being stirred up by the voices—that is, by the negative ways we see ourselves as participants in the event. It is clear that an early loss, such as the one Arlene experienced, would make someone feel sad, angry, and fearful. However, when these natural feelings are contaminated by emotions that have been triggered by the voice, depression can be the result. Therefore, it is important for us to make a distinction between these two emotions—that is, sadness and depression.

Many people mistake the experience of sad feelings for depression. However, there are significant differences between the two states. Experiencing feelings of sadness tends to put us in touch with ourselves and makes us feel more whole. On the other hand, if we are down or depressed, we may feel a mixture of unresolved grief, guilt, and anger, which we turn against ourselves. Many people are hesitant to experience deep feelings of sadness. If we anticipate feeling sad, we may feel tense, and fear we will become depressed, whereas actually experiencing our sad feelings often brings relief and makes us feel more unified and strong within ourselves.

How Do Depressed Adults Describe Their Experience?

Recently, a number of celebrities have broken through the stigma that has long been attached to depression and revealed how they had felt when they were depressed. In *On the Edge of Darkness: Conversations about Conquering Depression* (Cronkite 1994), some of these celebrities alluded to the distortions and vicious self-attacks of the critical inner voice that they experienced when they felt the most hopeless. Actor Rod Steiger, who had several bouts with depression, wrote:

> When you're depressed, it's as though this committee has taken over your mind, leaving you one depressing thought after the other. You don't shave, you don't shower, you don't brush your teeth. You don't care. . . . Part of the depression is as though you're punishing yourself for something. . . . Your sense of self, your appreciation for yourself, your respect for yourself, disappears completely. It certainly isn't that your mind goes blank. On the contrary, when you're depressed, your mind beats you to death with thoughts. It never stops.

[Your friends say,] "Your wife loves you, your child loves you, we're worried about you."

"They don't understand," the tired voice says. That's the wallowing in self-pity. "They don't understand." (46–48)

Television anchorwoman Kathy Cronkite described her own depression in the following terms:

I saw the world through dark-tinted glasses—my house was a wreck, my children monsters, my marriage in trouble, my body fat, my wardrobe ugly, my work without merit, and on and on. "I can't stand this, I can't stand feeling this way," I thought a million times. (9)

A writer who did not wish her real name disclosed had this to say:

People who have never experienced depression cannot imagine what it feels like, the hopelessness. Nothing helps you to feel better. Nothing. The ordinary things of life—a movie, a good meal, company, a walk, a beautiful painting—make you feel worse because they enhance how detached you are from the real world, how much I wasn't able to partake of the banquet in front of me. There is a great line from *Auntie Mame*: "Life is a banquet, most people are starving." I use it all the time. (34)

At the time he became depressed, Mike Wallace (of *Sixty Minutes*) was being sued by General Westmoreland. Wallace recalls how he felt:

The first three months were the plaintiff making his case. I'd pick up the paper every day, and they were saying "cheat, liar, fraud," et cetera. After a while I began to feel that way; you suddenly say to yourself, "Well, yeah, they're right." I still didn't know what it was. I thought I was just down. I remember we used to go to restaurants, and I'd say, "Everybody's pointing at me, the cheat, the fraud, the fake." You really believe these things! Astonishing! (14)

In recalling the lowest point in your life (or the lowest points) that you described in exercise 7.1, can you remember how you felt? What emotions were aroused as you began thinking negatively? What thoughts did you have that contributed to your feeling more and more down? How did they go? Did you act in a manner that was a result of these thoughts? Did any of the actions you took support these negative perceptions of yourself and your world? Do you remember a time when you turned against yourself and started believing very negative yet inaccurate things about yourself and others? What behaviors did you engage in that made the negative perceptions seem more real?

Exercise 7.2: Depression:
Your Critical Inner Voices and Your Feelings

To complete the second step in your exploration of traumatic or painful events in your life, begin by reviewing the negative thoughts you recorded in the middle column of exercise 7.1. On the left-hand side of the page of Exercise 7.2, record the critical inner voices that were the most intense or those that you feel had the most impact on your feelings after the triggering event or events. Next, on the right-hand side of the page, describe the emotions that you recall feeling when you experienced these thoughts.

An Example of Exercise 7.2

Here is another excerpt from Arlene's journal:

My critical inner voices contributing to depression	How these voices left me feeling
"It's your fault she died."	I felt extremely guilty. I was also ashamed, actually mortified, to feel relieved that she was dead, that I didn't have to take care of her anymore. I felt secretive, like I had committed a horrendous crime. I was terrified that someone would find out and I would be punished.
"What makes you think you can take care of your brother?"	I felt so nervous, so incompetent about taking care of him. But I was also furious and resentful. Why should I have to spend all my time watching my little brother and miss out on my own life?

The Continuum of Self-Destructive Behaviors and Critical Inner Voices

Based on extensive clinical findings, Robert Firestone (1988) proposed that negative thoughts vary along a continuum of intensity from mild self-criticisms to malicious self-accusations to thoughts influencing physically harmful behaviors. Similarly, self-defeating destructive behaviors exist on a parallel continuum ranging from self-denial to substance abuse and other self-destructive behaviors, culminating under certain conditions even in suicide.

Critical inner voices vary in content, in the intensity of the anger associated with them, and in the frequency with which we experience them. The negative thoughts that influence our self-defeating and self-destructive actions can be categorized under three main levels of self-punishing thoughts lying along the continuum, as follows:

The first level is made up of critical thoughts toward yourself: the types of negative thoughts that lead to low self-esteem, as described in chapter 2. People who are experiencing this level of negative thinking may act out a number of behaviors that support their negative self-image. For example, they may restrict pleasurable experiences, avoid involvement in relationships, or isolate themselves. They may also experience many negative attitudes toward other people; these attitudes are often cynical and hostile, and can lead those who have them to hurt others emotionally.

This level of critical thought appears to be a result of our internalizing both our parents' negative attitudes toward us and the unreasonable or age-inappropriate expectations they may have had of us. For example, a mother in one of our parenting classes believed that her six-month-old infant cried intentionally, just to get under her skin. In reality, infants lack the precognition necessary for intentional behavior. When parents hold such beliefs, they will tend to be angry at the infant and their behavior will be inappropriate in relation to their child's age. Statements such as *"You're too old to cry. You're such a bother!"* reflect these inaccurate assumptions about a child's capabilities. Children take these unrealistic expectations and judgmental attitudes into themselves in the form of self-critical thoughts and attitudes.

The second level of self-attack consists of thoughts that support or promote self-soothing behaviors—that is, actions that are carried out for the purpose of numbing our feelings. These include addictive behaviors such as overeating, anorexia, bulimia, drinking, drug use, excessive TV watching, compulsive exercising, or other routines that reduce tension and relieve pain. As noted, many of these behaviors are often an imitation of our parents' behaviors and lifestyles.

The third level of critical inner voices involves thoughts such as: *"You are a burden to everyone. Your family would be better off without you"* or *"Nothing matters anymore. You should just give up."* These thoughts lead to a sense of hopelessness and detachment from ourselves. This level of self-attack also includes thoughts encouraging us to engage in extreme risk-taking behavior and acts of self-harm. These critical inner voices may direct us to behave in ways that jeopardize our physical body, to be careless, or even to attack ourselves physically. At the extreme end of the continuum are destructive thoughts that, in certain cases, urge a person to plan the details of suicide or to actually kill himself or herself.

These negative thoughts are seriously self-destructive in nature. They appear to stem from parents' covert or overt aggression. At this level, a person has become identified with the punishing parent and has taken on that anger toward himself or herself. As described in chapter 1, when children are under unusual stress, they identify with the punishing parent and take in the hostile attitudes and angry feelings that the parent is experiencing at that moment. Later, as adults, they tend to unleash that same anger toward themselves in the form of self-destructive thoughts that can sometimes lead to actual self-harm.

To understand why we would give up our identity and take on the point of view of our parents, it is important to realize that children have a stronger *memory trace* (that is, a more enduring memory) for negative events than for positive ones. This seems to be a natural, innate human tendency.

For example, a father took his three children on a two-week camping trip. The father's recollection of the vacation was completely positive; he remembered sitting around the campfire with his kids singing and telling stories, hiking and fishing with his son, and so on. In telling the story of the trip to a friend, he described all the fun activities he and his children had enjoyed together. In contrast, the strongest memory about the vacation that his ten-year-old son reported was of the time his father yelled at him in the campground. He recalled the fear and humiliation he suffered that evening much more vividly than any of the enjoyable activities his father had recalled.

Exercise 7.3: You and the Continuum of Self-Destructive Thoughts

This exercise is designed to help you identify your critical inner voices at each level on the continuum. On the left-hand side of the page, write the critical inner voices you have at each level on the continuum. For level 1, you might want to refer back to exercise 2.2, for example, *"You're a failure. Can't you do anything right?"* or *"You're so unattractive."* For level 2, you might want to refer back to the left-hand column of exercise 6.2, for example, *"It's okay to take a hit, you'll be more relaxed"* or, later, *"You jerk, you never live up to your resolutions!"* For level 3, try to identify the critical inner voices you have that are seriously self-destructive, for example, *"What's the use? Nothing matters anymore"* or *"Stay away from your friends, you make them feel bad."* On the right-hand side of the page, identify any behaviors you engage in based on these thoughts; for example, thoughts that try to influence you to isolate yourself, soothe yourself compulsively, or engage in risk-taking behaviors or actions that are physically harmful.

How the Critical Inner Voice Influences You to Hold Back Pleasure and Happiness

There are a wide range of critical inner voices that urge people to give up the interests and activities that they particularly enjoy. This tendency to give up excitement in life is built into our defense system and can become a problem at an early age. Many of us prematurely restrict our lives or put limits on our experiences, often those that bring us the most pleasure and satisfaction.

Self-denial, this holding back of satisfying experiences from ourselves, is often looked on with favor and approval in our society; it is supported by many people's attitudes about age-appropriate roles and activities. The negative thoughts that many people experience are directly connected with patterns of self-denial. Many people, as they get older, gradually disengage from an active life. They participate less in sports and physical activities, have less interest in sex, and lose contact with old friends. They may tell themselves: *"You're crazy to still play sports at your age. People will think you're just trying to act young"* or *"Whoever heard of falling in love at your age?"* or *"Why bother to plan building a new house now? You probably won't be around to enjoy it."*

Although this form of self-denying behavior is not limited to people over forty, society's attitudes and even many of its institutions support the view that we should give up energetic activities as we grow older.

Combating Critical Inner Voices That Lead to Depression

The most powerful weapon in our arsenal for fighting against depression is to first become aware of the negative thoughts and self-critical attitudes that contribute to our feeling this way. If we are used to following the advice of the critical inner voice about seemingly less important things in life, we will become more susceptible to thoughts urging us to engage in more dangerous, self-destructive behaviors. Surrendering our own point of view, giving in, and listening to the dictates of the inner voice over time gives it power. The more we indulge in feeling like a bad person and engaging in behaviors that support this belief, the more entrenched it becomes.

For example, consider the following scenario: You have recently become aware that you gradually have given up an activity that used to interest you. You begin to realize that you are more indifferent to life and cynical about other people than you used to be. Looking back, you recall that at a certain point (weeks, months, or years before), you started adjusting your behavior to obey a voice that told you: *"Why bother going out with your friends? Why not stay home and watch TV by yourself? It's more relaxing."* Now you find yourself thinking hopeless thoughts like: *"What does it matter anyway? Nothing matters really. Your life is empty, you don't have any friends anymore, so who would care if you weren't around?"*

You can see how important it is to identify the voices early on, before things go to an extreme. It is also crucial to challenge any distorted beliefs about yourself that you tend to hold on to. Finally, you need to take the actions necessary to begin to move out of a depressed or blue mood as soon as you recognize the feelings and thoughts we have described in this chapter.

Identify the Critical Inner Voices That Influence Self-Denial and Giving Up

Identifying the voices that you hear when you limit pleasurable or meaningful experiences is an important step in challenging this deceptive enemy. Be aware of any seemingly friendly voices that influence self-denying patterns, which can lead to giving up on things that really matter to you.

Exercise 7.4: The Firestone Voice Scale for Self-Denying and Giving-Up Thoughts

Completing the scale in this exercise can help bring the contents of these self-denying thoughts more into the foreground of your thinking and under your conscious control.

Exercise 7.5: How Your Critical Inner Voice Rationalizes Self-Denial and Giving Up/What You Realistically Think

On the left-hand side of exercise 7.5, write down any thoughts (seemingly positive ones as well as negative ones) that urge you to deny yourself or that you use as a rationalization for not doing something you know you really enjoy. Next, on the right-hand side of the page, write a statement or statements to counteract these self-denying thoughts. Once you have actually written down the excuses that you use to limit your pleasure and happiness, you may be surprised to find out how ridiculous they are.

An Example of Exercise 7.5

Your excuses for denying yourself, and your rational responses, might look something like this:

What my critical inner voice says	What I realistically think
"Look at all the work you have to do. You can't afford to take time off."	I could work a little late tonight and take some time off tomorrow. Work isn't everything! I do need some time to relax.
"You don't deserve to have fun."	That's silly! Of course I do. Everybody deserves a chance to have fun and enjoy life.
"You're too old to have romance in your life."	No one's ever too old for love and romance.
"You should just give up. It's no use anymore."	I don't want to give up. I really care about my life.

Identify the Critical Inner Voices That Influence You to Be Alone and Isolated

When people gradually withdraw from close friends or loved ones and seek isolated activities or solitude, they become more cut off from their feelings. Sometimes they are involved in obsessive ruminations and voice attacks which make them feel bad about themselves and alienated from others.

Many people listen to a critical inner voice telling them that privacy and isolation are necessary. These thoughts are difficult to counter because they appear reasonable. Obviously we do need some degree of privacy for creative or concentrated work. However, extended periods of isolation from social contact with others can be detrimental to mental health.

For example, in one case, a woman who came close to dying from a serious suicide attempt reported that prior to her self-destructive act, her voice told her: *"You never have any time for yourself, to do what you want to do. You need some time alone so you can think."* However, once she was alone, she began planning the details of her suicide. In looking back, she realized that suicidal thoughts had not occurred to her when she was among friends, yet she had felt compelled by her critical inner voice to seek isolation, where she was at the mercy of vicious self-attacks and suicidal urges.

There may be times when you need to be alone. But if you find yourself spending long periods of time alone thinking self-critical thoughts, or worrying about a situation over which you have very little control, isolation could be a self-destructive choice for you.

Exercise 7.6: The Firestone Voice Scale for Isolation

To become more aware of critical inner voices you have experienced urging you to isolate yourself, fill out the questionnaire in this exercise.

Exercise 7.7: How Your Critical Inner Voice Influences Isolation/What You Realistically Think

In exercise 7.7, identify the voices you hear that encourage you to isolate yourself. On the left-hand side of the page, record the negative thoughts that urge you to be isolated and to spend extended periods of time alone. On the right-hand side, write down what you realistically think of those urges.

How Listening to Your Critical Inner Voice Can Move You Down the Continuum

The critical inner voices range in intensity from those that urge us to give up the activities we love the most to vicious attacks for even having simple wants and needs. Many people who follow the dictates of their voices for years without challenging them often fail to recognize the profound effect these attacks are having on their lives, or to see that they have become more susceptible to the seriously destructive voices that lie at the extreme end of the continuum. If we reach a point in life where we become demoralized from years spent listening to these voices and then suddenly wake up to the emptiness of our lives, we may experience the feelings of existential guilt described in chapter 2. This guilt often takes the form of self-recriminations promoted by the critical inner voice. The cycle of despair and hopelessness that follows can lead to more serious types of self-destructive actions.

As the voice becomes more intense and malicious, the anger and rage that people often begin to feel directed toward them make them feel agitated, in psychological pain, and desperate to get out of that pain. They may think to themselves: *"You scum! You reject! You're worthless! You don't deserve anything!"* In addition, when people accept the viewpoint of the critical inner voice, they no longer see themselves accurately. In other words, they cannot distinguish between a realistic, congenial view of themselves and a destructive, negative view of themselves. Thus, it is actually dangerous to accept core negative beliefs about ourselves without challenging them each time they come up.

If we suffer a major loss, setback, or other unfavorable circumstance, we may turn on ourselves before we realize that we are seeing the event in an exaggerated negative light. In reacting to a painful situation, we may rapidly descend down the continuum of negative thoughts and actions. At this point, we may begin to experience some of the emotions reported by people who have been seriously depressed. Yet it is possible for us to have almost no idea of how we got to this low point. Ironically, when we are hurting from a loss, we are perhaps the most susceptible to the critical inner voice, since it can play on these painful feelings and interpret them to its own advantage. The voice may exaggerate any shortcomings or faults we have and may amplify every contribution we have made to the problem. *"That's just the way I am"* is a common theme of people who have come to believe what the voice is telling them about themselves.

As described earlier, the depressed person has reached a stage where the point of view represented by the voice actually becomes the person's own point of view. A seriously depressed person has sided with the critical inner voice, believing its criticisms and acting on its commands, creating a life that really is depressing. We no longer vacillate between seeing life from our own viewpoint and seeing it from the point of view of the enemy within. In other words, we are now aligned more against ourselves than for ourselves and wholeheartedly believe everything our voice tells us. As a result, we no longer have contact with our real self and may feel hopelessly alienated from the people closest to us as well.

The voice is deceptive and seemingly logical. Another trick that it can play on us during this downward spiral is to try to convince us that our family and friends would be better off without us. It may attack us, saying: *"You've caused so much trouble to your family already. They would be happy to be rid of you for good."* This belief can become firmly entrenched in our thinking, yet it is never true. Family members never feel better when a loved one dies and in the case of suicide, they are devastated.

Steps for Challenging Depression

To combat the voices that contribute to depression, it is helpful to:

1. Identify and challenge the negative thoughts and beliefs you experience early in the self-destructive cycle.

2. Talk to a close friend who tends to have a more optimistic outlook. Talking to someone who is also down or cynical about life can actually make you feel worse.

3. Force yourself to engage in activities that you have found pleasurable in the past. Even if they don't seem appealing right now, they will help you start to overcome the apathy, indifference, and lack of energy that are major symptoms of depression.

Identify Thoughts That Can Lead to Depression

People who are depressed have patterns of negative thinking that, unless identified, exert more and more influence over their behavior and mood. For this reason, it is crucial that you become aware of what your critical inner voice is telling you and how it is affecting your behavior.

Exercise 7.8: The Firestone Voice Scale for Depression

The scale in exercise 7.8 is made up of negative thoughts that people experience when they are feeling down or depressed. Do any of these resonate with you? This can be an aid in identifying your thoughts that contribute to depression. Check the frequency with which you have experienced each of these self-destructive thoughts.

Exercise 7.9: Critical Inner Voices of Depression: Your Critical Inner Voice/The Real You

On the left-hand side of the page in exercise 7.9, write down any self-destructive thoughts you have that contribute to your giving up activities you enjoy, or isolating yourself, or any angry, vicious, name-calling thoughts you may direct against yourself. On the right-hand side of the page, write down your realistic, compassionate point of view.

It is important to realize that even if you have experienced some of the more extreme thoughts in exercise 7.8 (those that lie near the extreme end of the continuum), this does not necessarily mean that you are currently depressed or suicidal. However, if you are currently experiencing thoughts that you feel are seriously self-destructive, it is time for you to seek professional help. It is very important to share these thoughts with someone who can help you deal with them more effectively (see chapter 8, "How to Select a Therapist").

Some of the thoughts may be similar to those you experienced when you went through a particularly difficult time in your life, and you may no longer be experiencing them. However, it is a good idea to directly challenge any of these negative thoughts that still arise whenever you do become upset or are stressed.

Talk About Your Thoughts and Feelings with a Trusted Friend

Talk with a close and trusted friend about your negative thoughts, because speaking the voice aloud to another person gives you the opportunity to subject these self-attacks to reality testing. Don't choose a friend who is depressed or generally holds a cynical view of the world. You need to talk with a person who will not overly sympathize with your problems or commiserate with you. You don't want someone who will offer false reassurances, either. Select someone who is not critical or judgmental, but who will be honest. Try to find a person who is aware of his or her own negative thoughts and who understands the danger of listening to them.

Perhaps you can ask your friend to read the first chapter of this book prior to talking with you. It is a good idea to pick someone who will simply listen with an open mind and an empathic attitude while you reveal your critical inner voices. Most important, choose a person who feels more congenial toward you than you feel toward yourself when you are in a depressed mood. Ideally, your friend will be able to give you realistic, compassionate feedback regarding the negative beliefs you have that are incorrect. Someone who has a good sense of humor can also do much to help you see how ridiculous some of your negative beliefs are.

Don't be afraid or ashamed to admit how bad you actually feel. Talk about deep-seated beliefs you may have held about yourself for a long time. Share the critical inner voices you have been ashamed of in the past. You may find that you experience feelings of sadness as you begin to realize how long you have been listening to—and believing—things your voice has been telling you.

Become More Active to Counter Depression: Engage in Activities That Are Pleasurable to You

Physical activities that give us pleasure or reduce tension are effective antidotes to depression. When planning a new activity, it is important that you realize that you are eventually going to feel better as a result of doing this. Initially, your motivation may be low. This is understandable, because people who are even mildly depressed often feel so exhausted that they cannot even imagine the kinds of activities that might give them pleasure. They may not even be able to recall the activities, games, sports, or social events that they enjoyed before they became depressed.

It is important that you select a pleasant and rewarding activity that you truly enjoy, not something that would objectively be seen as a chore or a drudgery. As you become more energetic, you can begin to include in your routine activities that involve the practicalities of everyday living.

Write a list of the pleasurable activities that you had fun doing in the past. For example, you may have found art exciting and fulfilling—or photography; or individual sports such as swimming, running, roller blading, ice-skating, or skiing; or team sports and games; or boating; or travel; or taking an evening class; or visiting friends.

When people are down, their motivation, interest, and initiative are largely under the control of the critical inner voice. Therefore, once you have chosen an activity, it is valuable to explore the thoughts and beliefs that prevent you from taking action.

Exercise 7.10: Plan of Pleasurable Activities

In exercise 7.10, record the activity you are planning to engage in on the left-hand side of the page. Take time each week to write down on the right-hand side of the page any negative thoughts that are trying to talk you out of participating in the activity.

If you doggedly continue to engage in the activity you have selected, you will gradually and steadily reduce the power the voice has had over you. For example, before she became depressed, Teresa had enjoyed hiking. So she decided to begin vigorously walking twenty minutes every day to help her cope with her depressed mood. After several weeks, she reported:

> Since I started feeling better, I've had this image of my voice as an evil witch, sort of like the Wicked Witch of the West in *The Wizard of Oz*. It's really clear to me now that if I stand up to the voice by continuing to walk every day in spite of its yelling at me in my head, it loses its power over me. It's like the scene in the movie where Dorothy throws a bucket

of water on the witch. The witch starts shrieking and yelling and quickly melts away to nothing. Actually she ends up as a tiny dark spot of water on the floor. That's exactly what's happened to my voices, the ones that used to see everything in a gloomy, dark light; they've been reduced to a little echo of negative thinking that I know still exists somewhere in the back of my mind, but which is not active or controlling me the way it used to do.

Continually challenging the thoughts that were making you feel lethargic or passive by simply going ahead with your plans no matter how you feel will often lead to a renewed interest in life and will likely increase your energy level. You will gradually recover your own initiative and motivation, which in turn will help you maintain a more active life.

When people retreat from seeking gratification in the real world with real people, they gradually become increasingly more indifferent to life and give up more and more areas of experience that they once found pleasurable and worthwhile. Seriously depressed people become listless and apathetic as a result of trying to struggle against their self-abusive thoughts. They no longer have an accurate view of themselves; in fact, they cannot tell the difference between a realistic view of themselves and negative views that they have accepted since childhood.

Externalizing the critical inner voices—bringing them out into the light of day—can help dispel a depressed state. To do this, it is important to (1) identify and challenge your core negative beliefs about yourself and the world and any thoughts that trigger feelings of hopelessness, helplessness, and despair; (2) talk openly about these beliefs and thoughts with a trusted, caring friend to help regain your own point of view; and (3) engage in activities that give you pleasure and renewed energy.

The exercises in this chapter can help you to increase your awareness of your self-destructive internal dialogue and of the particular events and situations that are likely to trigger your self-attacks. Most important, exposing the dictates of your critical inner voice will enable you to gradually take power over it and move toward choices that more closely correspond to your goals, interests, and priorities. You can use these methods as an ongoing form of self-investigation as you pursue your personal development and embark on a life of continuous change.

Exercise 7.1: Depression and Life Events: Your Critical Inner Voice/The Real You

Triggering event	Critical inner voices I recall experiencing at the time of the event	My realistic thoughts about the event *now*

Exercise 7.2: Depression:
Your Critical Inner Voices and Your Feelings

My critical inner voices contributing to depression   **How these voices left me feeling**

_____   _____

_____   _____

_____   _____

_____   _____

_____   _____

_____   _____

_____   _____

_____   _____

_____   _____

_____   _____

_____   _____

_____   _____

Exercise 7.3: You and the Continuum of Self-Destructive Thoughts

My critical inner voices

Behaviors I engage in

Level 1: *Thoughts that lead to low self-esteem and self-defeating behavior*

Level 1:

_____

_____

_____

_____

_____

_____

_____

_____

Level 2: *Thoughts that support the cycle of addiction*

Level 2:

_____

_____

_____

_____

_____

_____

_____

_____

Level 3: *Thoughts that lead to seriously self-destructive behavior*

Level 3:

_____

_____

_____

_____

_____

_____

Exercise 7.4: The Firestone Voice Scale for Self-Denying and Giving-Up Thoughts

Circle the frequency with which you experience the following critical inner voices:

0 = Never   1 = Rarely   2 = Once in a while   3 = Frequently   4 = Most of the time

0 1 2 3 4   You'll save money if you don't take this trip.

0 1 2 3 4   It's too much trouble to go out to dinner. Just stay home.

0 1 2 3 4   You don't deserve happiness. You're such a creep!

0 1 2 3 4   What's so exciting about playing baseball or football or dancing (or any activity)? You should just relax and settle down.

0 1 2 3 4   Look at all the work you have to do. You can't afford to take time off.

0 1 2 3 4   You've always had problems with sex. You should just give it up.

0 1 2 3 4   Why bother trying to get a date? If you don't date, you'll have more time to study.

0 1 2 3 4   Just look at how your friends are acting. They're so immature. They think they're having fun, but they're really just making fools of themselves. Don't be like them!

0 1 2 3 4   You shouldn't be out having fun with all the misery in the world.

0 1 2 3 4   You're too old to have romance in your life.

0 1 2 3 4   What's all this passion in your relationship? You should just settle down.

0 1 2 3 4   Nothing matters anymore.

0 1 2 3 4   Why bother even trying?

0 1 2 3 4   Nothing is any fun anymore.

0 1 2 3 4   Why bother making friends?

0 1 2 3 4   What's the use? What's the point of anything really?

0 1 2 3 4   Your work doesn't matter. Why bother even trying? Nothing matters anyway.

Exercise 7.5: How Your Critical Inner Voice Rationalizes Self-Denial and Giving Up/What You Realistically Think

What my critical inner voices says

What I realistically think

_____   _____

_____   _____

_____   _____

_____   _____

_____   _____

_____   _____

_____   _____

_____   _____

_____   _____

_____   _____

_____   _____

_____   _____

_____   _____

_____   _____

_____   _____

_____   _____

Exercise 7.6: The Firestone Voice Scale for Isolation

Circle the frequency with which you experience the following critical inner voices:

0 = Never   1 = Rarely   2 = Once in a while   3 = Frequently   4 = Most of the time

0 1 2 3 4   Wouldn't it be great to go off by yourself and be able to read or watch TV with no one interrupting?

0 1 2 3 4   It's been so tense at work. You need to go off by yourself.

0 1 2 3 4   Why go out with your friends tonight? You could just stay at home and relax.

0 1 2 3 4   You need to get away so you can think about things.

0 1 2 3 4   It's so irritating to have to be around people all day.

0 1 2 3 4   The only way you can relax is to be by yourself.

0 1 2 3 4   You need more space, more time for yourself.

0 1 2 3 4   These aren't your kind of people. Why don't you go off by yourself?

0 1 2 3 4   It's such a hassle to go to that party. You have to get dressed up and put up a front. Why don't you just stay home?

0 1 2 3 4   You're no fun to be around. You should just stay by yourself.

Exercise 7.7: How Your Critical Inner Voice Influences Isolation/What You Realistically Think

What my critical inner voices say

What I realistically think

_____   _____

_____   _____

_____   _____

_____   _____

_____   _____

_____   _____

_____   _____

_____   _____

_____   _____

_____   _____

_____   _____

_____   _____

_____   _____

_____   _____

_____   _____

Exercise 7.8: The Firestone Voice Scale for Depression

Circle the frequency with which you experience the following critical inner voices:

0 = Never   1 = Rarely   2 = Once in a while   3 = Frequently   4 = Most of the time

0 1 2 3 4	You just don't belong anywhere.
0 1 2 3 4	You're a horrible person! You don't deserve anything.
0 1 2 3 4	Just look at yourself in the mirror! You're so ugly. No one can stand you!
0 1 2 3 4	The world is a real mess. Why should you care about anything?
0 1 2 3 4	Your friends really hate you.
0 1 2 3 4	Your life is so boring and empty.
0 1 2 3 4	Don't ever get too happy, because the ax is bound to fall.
0 1 2 3 4	You should just smash your hand, you creep! You deserve everything that happens to you.
0 1 2 3 4	Nobody really likes you. You're an unlovable person.
0 1 2 3 4	You deserve all the bad things that are happening to you.
0 1 2 3 4	Don't you see what effect you have on your family? Can't you see how you make them feel?
0 1 2 3 4	You're always stirring up trouble, bothering people. Why can't you just stay away?
0 1 2 3 4	You don't care for anybody. You've never cared for anybody in your whole life!
0 1 2 3 4	Don't show anybody how bad you feel.
0 1 2 3 4	Who do you think you are, anyway? You're nothing!
0 1 2 3 4	Who could love you? You have nothing to offer.
0 1 2 3 4	You don't deserve anything.
0 1 2 3 4	Your family would be better off without you. Just stay away, it's the only decent thing to do.

Exercise 7.9: Critical Inner Voices of Depression: Your Critical Inner Voice/The Real You

What my critical inner voices say

What I realistically think

Exercise 7.10: Plan of Pleasurable Activities

The activities I plan to engage in

A weekly report of my critical inner voices about my plan

_____

_____

_____

_____

_____

_____

_____

_____

_____

_____

_____

_____

Chapter 8

How to Select a Therapist

The psychotherapeutic alliance is a unique human relationship, wherein a devoted and trained person attempts to render assistance to another person. . . . Nowhere in life is a person listened to, felt, and experienced with such concentrated sharing and emphasis on every aspect of personal communication. . . . To the extent that a new fantasy bond or illusion of connection is formed (for example, doctor-patient, therapist-client, parent-child), the relationship will be detrimental; whereas in a situation that is characterized by equality, openness, and true compassion, there will be movement toward personal growth in both parties.

—Robert W. Firestone

If you feel that what you have learned about yourself from reading this book has been valuable, but you believe that you could benefit from additional help, you may want to consider psychotherapy. Or you may choose to use therapy as a tool to continue the process of change and personal growth you have begun. In either case, there are many capable therapists from whom to choose. Therapists use a variety of methods that are based on a wide range of psychological theories.

Most of these methods have been found to be successful in helping people learn how to better deal with problems in living.

An effective psychotherapy sensitively challenges people's defense systems and helps them regain feeling for themselves. It exposes the critical inner voice and counters its influence on the patient's behavior and lifestyle. Ideally, it takes place in the context of an equal interaction between patient and therapist.

Factors to Consider in Making Your Choice

How can you choose the right therapist for you? There are a number of questions you can ask yourself during and after the initial session, and before making your final decision: "Did I feel comfortable with this person? Are we compatible? Did I feel really listened to and understood? Did I have a sense that this was going to be a safe place to explore my thoughts, feelings, and deepest concerns?"

You can generally trust your intuitive feelings in considering whether to work with an individual. The following are other important questions to reflect upon:

- Did the therapist seem like a real person to you? Or did he or she seem to be playing some kind of role?

- Did the therapist draw you out and make you feel like talking about yourself?

- Did it appear that your story had an impact on the therapist?

- Did you feel heard by the therapist when telling your story or stating your point of view?

- Did you feel that the therapist had respect for you as a person and was not condescending?

- Did the therapist say anything that tended to distract you from feeling?

- Was the therapist more passive in his or her approach, or did he or she take an active part in the conversation? Which approach do you prefer?

- Was the therapist friendly and warm, yet sensitive to the boundaries inherent in the therapy setting?

- Did the therapist seem to have an optimistic outlook on life?

- Did you sense that the therapist would be open to hearing all of your feelings, even if they were angry feelings expressed toward him or her?

- Did you feel better or worse after your first meeting?

During your first meeting, feel free to ask your potential therapist whatever you feel you need to know in order to make your decision. The following are questions you may consider asking regarding the therapist's preferred type of therapy and techniques.

- What does the therapist see as the goal of therapy?

- How does the therapist's goal or goals for therapy resonate with what you want to get out of the process?

- What is the therapist's approach? What methods does he or she plan to employ?

- How long will the course of therapy last? How many sessions does the therapist consider as necessary or optimal for you?

- What does the therapist expect from you? Are there homework assignments involved? Or any other expectations of you between sessions? Are you comfortable with these expectations?

A therapist who is effective and compatible with one person may not be with another person. Your friend or family member who recommended this therapist may feel compatible with his or her approach, yet you may not. If your concerns are complex and long-standing, you want to choose a therapist who has extensive experience and training. The expertise and access to resources that such an individual would have could facilitate your receiving the help you need.

Personal Qualities of the Therapist That Are Conducive to Good Therapy

Research has found that the relationship between the patient and the therapist is one of the most important elements contributing to good outcomes in therapy. The primary factor determining whether therapy will be helpful to you is not the type of therapy your therapist practices, but rather the level of genuine relating your therapist is willing and able to offer.

The therapist who is able to provide you with a safe, caring atmosphere is likely to be an effective therapist. But what specific personal qualities and behaviors are ideal for a therapist to possess? The following is a summary of the ideal characteristics to look for in choosing a therapist.

The ideal therapist would be a person of unusual honesty and integrity. He or she would be sensitive and feelingful as well as empathic and understanding toward you. Although your therapist would have an optimistic outlook and a strong belief in the possibility of personal growth and change, he or she would not underestimate the strength of your defense system and would be sensitive to your fear of change.

Ideally, your therapist would be interested in and come to understand your innermost thoughts and feelings and would be aware of your unique methods of defense. He or she would be open to new ideas and real experiences in each therapy session and would be nondefensive about his or her mistakes and blind spots.

Your therapist would be able to see your strengths, positive qualities, and potentialities that may be covered over by defensive behaviors influenced by your critical inner voice. He or she would provide you with glimpses of the real you. Good therapists are able to communicate to their patients a vision of what their lives will be like as they become more vulnerable and less defended.

Effective therapists maintain an open and receptive attitude as they listen to their patients, and they strive to be honest as they respond to them. Because they serve as positive role models for their patients, they demonstrate through their behavior and responses that they have integrity—that is, that their words fit their actions and underlying feelings.

Therapists' integrity and strength of character partly come from an ability to accept their anger and use it effectively when necessary; for example, in confronting their patients' acting out of self-defeating or self-destructive behaviors. Ideally, they are aware of the numerous defensive behaviors that may be harmful to you and would have the strength and courage to help expose and interrupt these patterns.

An effective therapist does not set himself or herself apart from his or her patient as someone who is superior, but demonstrates by his or her behavior how to struggle against the critical inner voice and how to live less defensively. He or she shows compassion and respect for the patient's striving to live a better life and is usually able to predict at what points the patient will be experiencing anxiety or intensified voice attacks.

Your ideal therapist would suspend judgment or evaluation about what you are communicating, while exploring with you the important connections you make between your past experiences and your current problems. He or she would not be intrusive in his or her explanations or responses to what you are revealing in the session and would not presume to have special knowledge about the sources of your problems or your underlying feelings, thoughts, or motives. This is an important consideration, because an incorrect, ill-timed, or insensitive response on the part of a therapist can effectively discourage, or shut down altogether, a patient's desire to communicate his or her deepest concerns.

In summary, according to Beutler, Bongar, and Shurkin (1998), "an effective therapist is one who cares, is attentive, makes few critical judgments, doesn't interfere, and offers a level of activity that is consistent with the patient's particular expectations and preferences" (71).

The Therapeutic Relationship

Ideally, your therapist would offer you an authentic relationship—that is, be interested and compassionate as well as direct and responsible. He or she would be an ally as you move away from a self-protective lifestyle toward genuine relationships. Effective therapists are willing to talk openly about the therapy relationship. Often, they encourage their patients to discuss how they are feeling about the relationship, both positive and negative reactions. And they are receptive to expressions of their patients' anger and hostility.

A therapist who tends to be critical and who dwells on your faults and weaknesses can be destructive rather than helpful. In contrast, a therapist who acknowledges your strengths as frequently as your defensive behaviors and limitations can enhance your growth. A therapist who is disrespectful, caustic, or sarcastic will be disruptive to the therapeutic relationship. Therapists show disrespect by being late for their sessions, allowing interruptions, or forgetting relevant information about their patients. They may fail to attend closely to what their patients are revealing and, at the same time, inappropriately disclose personal information.

Ideally, your therapist would utilize the therapeutic relationship to help you recover your feelings for yourself and to implicitly teach you to value yourself as a unique individual. Through his or her interactions with you, he or she would be offering you the opportunity not only to develop as a person, but to learn to relate in a manner that is more fulfilling. You would then be able to apply what you have learned to enhance the quality of your present-day associations.

Finally, your therapist would be sensitive to the ways that people have been hurt early in their lives. He or she would be exceptionally skillful in helping you to reconnect to yourself and to your life. To achieve this goal, the good therapist must be sensitive to your real feelings, qualities, and priorities, and be able to distinguish them from the overlay on your personality (your critical inner voice) that has prevented you from reaching your full potential for living.

As you progress in therapy, you will discover that you no longer need to rely on the destructive, limiting defenses that have kept you alienated from your feelings. You will no longer feel compelled to repeat familiar, self-defeating patterns of behavior, which in turn will open the possibility for continuous change and development in your life. The therapeutic venture, by helping you recognize and gradually take power over the critical inner voice and its antifeeling, antilife prescriptions, offers you a unique opportunity to fulfill your human potentialities.

Part III

Guidelines for Living
the "Good Life"

This section explains what is meant by living the "good life"—that is, a life that is warmer, emotionally richer, and more fulfilling than what you may have experienced in the past. Chapter 9 has guidelines for optimal child development that address many of the issues people face in striving to be the best parents they can be. Chapter 10 describes ideas developed by Robert Firestone that are conducive to living a less defended and more fulfilling life, and ways of putting these ideas into practice in your everyday life.

Chapter 9

For Parents: Guidelines for Optimal Child Development

Individuals whose integrity has not been damaged in childhood, who were protected, respected, and treated with honesty by their parents, will be intelligent, responsive, empathic, and highly sensitive in both youth and adulthood. They will take pleasure in life and will feel no need to kill or even hurt others or themselves.

—Alice Miller

Today's parents are trying to raise healthy children under difficult, stressful conditions. Research has shown that it is optimal for children to have at least four or five caring adults to take a serious interest in them. However, many families are faced with circumstances that make this ideal an impossible dream. Often both parents are working hard to support their children and do not have trusted adults to rely on for help with child care. There are increasing numbers of single parents raising their children alone, without the assistance of even one other adult. In addition, American society, in contrast to many other industrialized societies, does not support parents by providing adequate child care for all families.

Aside from these outside pressures, the most significant problems we all face in raising children can be found in our families of origin. In order to be effective parents and develop secure attachments with our children, we need to make sense of what happened in our own childhoods. We need to face the painful feelings we experienced as a result of the treatment we received and regain feeling for ourselves as the unique individuals we are. In recognizing where our beliefs and feelings about children come from, we can gain more control over the defensive behaviors that we feel compelled to act out with our children.

Child rearing is a highly creative, challenging, and stressful task, and like other creative endeavors, this task requires considerable reflection and thought. Instead of having a rigid or restrictive image of what we want our children to become, we can learn ways of nurturing them and guiding them that would help them express their own natural qualities and unique ways of being. With this goal in mind, it is worthwhile to examine the conditions under which children develop a way of seeing themselves as bad or unlovable and to understand how they develop a critical inner voice.

In this chapter, we focus first on several painful disclosures of parents who had the courage to reveal what they really felt at times in interactions with their children. They honestly admitted feelings and behaviors that they considered to be unacceptable and that caused them to feel ashamed and guilty. They raised issues that most parenting books fail to discuss. Second, we provide guidelines and suggestions that may be helpful to parents in raising their children.

Repeating Our Parents' Behaviors

"I swore that I would treat my children differently than my parents treated me, but I find myself doing the exact same things they did." This parent is describing one of the most mystifying and distressing aspects of parenting. In spite of their best intentions, people find themselves acting in the same negative ways toward their children that their parents acted toward them. By understanding how and why negative parental traits are passed down through the generations, parents can gain control of this process and interrupt the cycle.

This transmission of parents' negative traits through the generations involves three phases:

1. To varying degrees, all of us suffered rejection, deprivation, hostility, and trauma in our formative years. At those times when our parents were out of control, either emotionally or physically, we took on the punishing parent's feelings, thoughts, and attitudes toward us in the form of a critical inner voice. In other words, we assumed the identity of our parents as they were at their worst, not as they usually were in their everyday lives.

2. We retained this hostile inner voice within us throughout our lives, restricting, limiting, and punishing ourselves, essentially parenting ourselves as we were parented.

3. When we become parents, we feel almost compelled to act out similar patterns of mistreatment on our children. During stressful interactions with our child, we may find ourselves saying and doing things we vowed we would never say or do. We almost find ourselves looking over our shoulder to see who said the words we have just uttered. Our child, in turn, takes in this outburst of punishing feelings and thoughts as a self-depreciating inner voice, thereby completing the cycle.

For example, in a parenting group, Samantha, fifty, revealed that when her daughter was small, she had often resented her because feeding and taking care of her took so much time and energy. She said:

> I hated that when she cried, I had to stop everything I was doing to feed her. It was something that could interrupt me at any time. She needed something and wanted something that I had to respond to, and I felt resentful when I was feeding her. Ever since then, I've felt really ashamed of those feelings. But I also know that I'm starting to see more clearly the way my mother was with me. Things that I've been vague about are starting to come out clear.
>
> I realize that today whenever I feel bad or down, I tell myself things like: *"Don't bother your husband with your problems. Don't bother your friends, stop bothering people. You're such a burden to people!"* But that's exactly the way my mother must have felt toward me, and so I saw my own daughter as a burden. I also remember that sometimes when she would cry, I actually wouldn't hear her—my husband or somebody would have to tell me she was crying, and so there was that time period when she was crying and I wasn't responding to her.

Julie, Samantha's twenty-two-year-old daughter, tended to deny her own wants and rarely expressed them. She described a critical inner voice that told her:

> *"Don't ask for anything. You don't deserve anything. Besides, you're so demanding, Just stay out of the way, stay in the background. Nobody wants to give you anything because you're not nice, and you're so demanding. You're a burden to your husband, to your friends, to everybody."*

After identifying the negative thoughts she had toward herself, Julie realized that she perceived her two-year-old son, Jake, in much the same way she had been seen by her mother. When she was trying to arrange child care for Jake, she often told herself:

> *"How could you ask anybody to watch him? He's so whiny, clingy, always wanting something. He's in an awful phase—the terrible twos—so how could*

you burden anyone with taking care of him? Just take care of him yourself and stop asking for help."

Children threaten their parents' defense system by reawakening painful feelings from the past. The innocence, liveliness, and spontaneity of a child can remind us of the hurts in our own childhood. Relating closely with our children threatens to reactivate these old hurts. In these interactions, we may experience anger or resentment toward our children without understanding why.

In addition, many parents experience considerable discomfort when their children pass through stages of development that were particularly painful or traumatic for the parents themselves. During these phases, parents often treat the child in a manner reminiscent of how they were treated at this age.

For example, in a parenting group, Ted spoke about his feelings for his four-year-old son, Charlie. Ted had wanted a child, specifically a son, for many years. He and his wife went to great lengths, consulting fertility experts and considering many options, before Charlie was finally born. Now Ted was tortured to find that he could not feel close to his son. Here is part of a dialogue between Ted and the parenting group's leader, Dr. Firestone:

Ted:　　　　　　I've noticed that I am much closer to adults than I am to Charlie. I have a kind of superstition in my mind that when he's older, I'll be able to get closer to him. So I've been searching to find out why that is. I had this thought that I was avoiding Charlie in the same way that I was avoided, and that I wouldn't give to him something that I didn't get for myself. Then I started to remember that my father wasn't there from the time that I was one to the time that I was four and a half.

Dr. Firestone:　The point you made was that painful feelings are aroused in you any time you treat Charlie or feel toward Charlie in a way that is different from the way you were treated. That seems to lead to a lot of pain for you. It somehow emphasizes the pain that you went through as a child yourself. So it's difficult to treat him with tenderness and sensitivity when in fact that was different from your own experience. Your father's absence tormented you; the way you described it, he avoided the family. In some way, you have developed the same pattern in relation to Charlie.

Ted:　　　　　　Yes, it's very rare that I ever have any real relations with Charlie. Mostly it's the relation of not being there, even when I'm there.

Dr. Firestone:　Even when you're in close quarters, you tend to be insulated, you're saying.

Ted: Right. I was really surprised to see that I'm actually better adapted to having feelings toward adults and even toward other children than toward Charlie.

Dr. Firestone: Why do you think that is?

Ted: Because I won't give to him what I didn't get myself.

Dr. Firestone: And that makes you feel sad.

Ted: It's a combination of shame and a wasted sadness. He's there wanting, just like I was there wanting, and there's no real reason. I don't even believe that I'm incapable, but I believe I'm acting irrationally.

Being loved and valued by their children can make parents feel a poignant, painful sadness that they find difficult to endure. Many pull away from their child after having this kind of close contact. In fact, the unwillingness of defended parents to allow their suppressed emotions to reemerge during tender moments with their children may be the major reason they find it difficult to sustain loving, affectionate relationships with their children.

Guilt About Not Always Feeling Love

"I don't feel loving feelings toward my child all the time," said a parent in a parenting group, reflecting a concern most parents experience. First, it is essential that all parents know that unconditional love does not exist. It is a myth that has become a basic part of our heritage and system of values. Second, belief in this unrealistic ideal contributes to feelings of guilt in parents because as human beings, they have limitations and weaknesses, and they are not perfect and completely loving. Therefore, it is absurd for parents to attack themselves for falling short of this ideal.

The ambivalent attitudes we have toward our children are simply a reflection of the ambivalent attitudes we have toward ourselves. The fact that we love our children and want to nurture them does not invalidate the resentment and other negative feelings we have at times toward them. Similarly, the fact that we sometimes have negative, hostile feelings toward our children does not negate our love or concern for them. We express ambivalent attitudes in all of our relationships to some degree. To the extent that we fail to recognize these conflicting attitudes toward ourselves and our children, we may be insensitive to our children and cause them unnecessary emotional pain. Only through developing compassion for ourselves and understanding how we learned the negative attitudes we have toward ourselves can we provide the warmth, affection, love, and control necessary for our children's well-being.

Many parents tend to deny weaknesses or unpleasant traits in themselves, perceiving them instead in a particular child, and then punish the imagined or exaggerated trait in the child. When this occurs, the child is basically being used as a waste receptacle or dumping ground for traits the parents attempt to disown in themselves. Often different children in a family are assigned different labels or are singled out to be "containers" for the projected traits of their parents.

If you find yourself feeling critical or punitive toward your child, it is helpful to ask yourself, "What am I angry at him (her) for? Why am I so angry? Does it really just have to do with him (her)? Could I have these feelings toward myself for these same things?"

For example, a mother with a prudish view about sex disowned sexual feelings in herself and instead continually worried about her daughter's emerging sexuality. Fearing that her daughter would become promiscuous as she reached her teens, she became obsessed with her daughter's activities, reading her e-mails and searching her belongings and schoolwork for clues that she was involved with boys. Later, when the girl attended college, she fulfilled her mother's predictions by becoming sexually involved with a number of men. In general, children accept the negative labels their parents assign to them, all the while maintaining an idealized view of the parents. They often become imprisoned for life in the narrow, restrictive labeling system that formed their identity within their family.

It is unfortunate that when children are damaged during their formative years, they often become difficult to like and love as they grow older. By the time they reach school age, many children are no longer the innocently loving and lovable creatures they once were. They may have been so bent out of shape that they have begun to exhibit negative behavior patterns and character traits such as whining, sulking, complaining, and manipulating. Contrary to popular opinion, these children are not simply "going through a phase."

It is more constructive for you to try to find out the cause of your children's disruptive behavior than to continually punish the behavior itself. For example, try to develop a sensitive interest in your child's arguments and expressions of sibling rivalry instead of allowing the infighting to continue. Unless they are understood and challenged, these offensive habits will persist and develop into more sophisticated defensive behaviors as your child reaches adolescence or adulthood.

If you are a parent with a child who is struggling with misbehavior, it may be helpful to ask yourself these questions: What is the child's behavior saying to you? Is he or she angry? Hurt? Frustrated? Scared? Do you think your child may be using this behavior to defend against pain or sadness? Are certain events currently affecting your child's mood or behavior? Are there certain behaviors that your child engages in that are unpleasant and make you angry at him or her? Do these behaviors reflect the ways you were seen or taught that children were? Have you talked with your child and attempted to find out what he or she is really feeling?

Unfortunately, many parents do not allow their children an opportunity to deal with distressing events. They discourage their children from expressing their painful reactions, whether by crying or by talking about their feelings. In this manner, parents often perpetuate their children's suffering. By not providing them with an outlet for dealing with their pain, they teach them to suppress their feeling reactions.

Guidelines for Child Rearing

The ultimate goal of parents is to help their children develop into decent, likable adults who enjoy the rewards of a well-balanced life. As stated throughout this chapter, regaining feeling about your own childhood experiences is the key element that will enable you to achieve this goal. In addition, there are some guidelines that can be of further help to you as a parent.

Avoid Unnecessary Rules

It is helpful for parents to avoid unnecessary restrictions, rules, and standards. It is remarkable how few rules or restrictions are really necessary to accomplish our goals of effectively socializing our children. Our goals as parents can be better realized when the rules we do make are about significant issues and are consistently upheld. Instead of having a direct confrontation on trivial issues, such as "You have to eat your vegetables or you can't have dessert," we can establish a limited number of rules and then firmly enforce them.

We need to clearly state our standards and rules to our children. As a child matures, we can explain the reasoning behind the rules and teach the importance of learning self-control. In situations where definite rules apply, we would not act as though our child has a choice in the matter. For example, if you set a specific bedtime for your six-year-old, obviously you would not ask him each night if he wanted to go to bed and then insist that he go anyway. You would simply exert your authority in a straightforward manner: "Now you are going to bed," not "Would you like to go to bed?"

Be a Positive Role Model

Psychologists have found that children really "do as parents do, not as they say." Being a positive role model for good behavior is far more powerful than specific training or disciplinary measures in raising children. These processes of identification and imitation overshadow any statements, rules, and prescriptions for good behavior. Children develop behaviors through observing their parents in day-to-day life. Every behavior that a parent engages in should be worthy of imitating, because children *will* imitate it.

If parents engage in behaviors that are influenced by the critical inner voice, their children are destined to mimic them as they grow older. These behaviors include playing the victim, self-denial or giving up pleasure and happiness, a pattern of addiction, passivity, dishonesty, phoniness, prejudice, vanity, tightness or lack of generosity, sarcasm, indifference, intrusiveness, and irritability, among others.

As you read the previous chapters, did you identify any personality traits or behaviors in yourself that you consider to be toxic or undesirable? Are these imitations of your parents' behaviors? Are your children imitating any of these ways of acting? Which traits or behaviors in yourself do you feel are most harmful in that your child will probably imitate them? Simply having an awareness of these issues often has a positive effect.

Exercise 9.1: The Firestone Voice Scale for Parents

Filling out the questionnaire in exercise 9.1 will help you become more aware of critical inner voices you are experiencing that are having an impact on how you parent.

Reward Rather than Punish Your Children

Psychologists have found that *positive reinforcement*, or reward, tends to increase the frequency of the behavior that is being rewarded. They have also found that *negative reinforcement*, or punishment, is not as effective in its ability to stop the expression of undesirable behaviors. Children respond positively to smiling, verbal praise, and physical affection. On the other hand, punishment tends to arouse negative emotions such as fear, shame, guilt, and anger. Children who are harshly punished rarely remember the object lesson, but do remember the fear they felt at the time they were being punished.

Parents who are continually nagging, complaining, or lecturing are usually unsuccessful in disciplining their children. These forms of punishment arouse the child's resentment and anger but fail to control his or her behavior. It is better to use a combination of approval, tangible rewards, genuine acknowledgment (not false praise or flattery), and some form of negative consequence for misbehavior. We suggest that parents not offer monetary rewards for good behavior, because this practice tends to place the child's behavior on a commercial basis rather than a personal one.

Avoid Physical Punishment

It is important to never spank, beat, or physically abuse a child. If you need to restrain a child, for example to keep him or her from running into the street, you can hold the child firmly and talk to him or her sternly or even move him or her physically to get him or her to go where you wish; you do not need to strike the child.

The more you develop as a person in your own life, the better able you will be to deal with your child's annoying behaviors. As parents come to accept and understand all their own feelings, including their angry feelings, they are better able to control the expression or acting out of aggressive behaviors toward their children.

Becoming more accepting of anger is a learning process that takes some time. You can learn strategies for dealing with your anger at those times you find your fuse is getting short. Parent educators recommend that you give yourself a cooling-off period: take a few steps back from your child, breathe deeply, and slowly count backward from twenty to zero. When you feel more in control of your anger, you can distract your child from the situation by listening to music or reading a story together.

It is also recommended that, if possible, you leave the situation in someone else's hands and take a break to calm down. This is one of the many reasons it is beneficial to include other interested and compassionate adults (family members or friends) in raising your children. It broadens your overall perspective on your child, and it is helpful to be able to share the responsibility of raising children with others. Sharing the emotional and physical care of the child can ease the pressures of parenting and help you become a more relaxed and effective parent.

Exercise 9.2: What Do You Think When You Are Angry at Your Child?

If you have problems with anger, you might want to write down your angry thoughts on the left-hand side of the page in exercise 9.2. Do any of these angry thoughts seem to reflect your own negative self-attitudes or critical inner voices? Write these down in the middle column. Do any of these thoughts remind you of things that were said to you as a child? Record these statements in the right-hand column.

For example, on the left-hand side of the page, one father wrote down a thought that expressed his irritation with his three-year-old son: "That kid is driving me crazy." He then recalled that when he was growing up, this was how his mother had described him to her friends and relatives. In addition, whenever she was really angry, she yelled at him so loud that the neighbors could hear, "You're driving me crazy!" In reflecting on this pattern of angry thinking, this father realized that he had numerous critical inner voices telling him, *"You're always making trouble. Why can't you just stay in the background? No one really likes you. You drive the people crazy at work. Why don't you just shut up!"* As you write down your angry thoughts and any negative voices you have about yourself, you may begin to recall situations in your childhood where you were treated harshly by a parent, relative, sibling, or teacher.

Avoid using idle threats of future punishment to enforce your rules. How many times have you heard parents repeatedly warning their children: "If you don't behave yourself, you won't get to go to the movies, or the park, or out to eat with us" or "If you don't stop what you're doing, you're going to get a spanking." Many parents threaten actions that they have no intention of taking, or in some other way fail to back up their threats with action. It is clear that threats that are not carried out are ineffective and undermine parents' authority. What you are teaching your child in these instances is that he or she can misbehave and there are no consequences.

Avoid Judgmental Attitudes

Judgmental or moralistic attitudes act to diminish a child's self-esteem. They tend to teach children that they are bad because they cry or feel sad, because they have needs, wants, and desires, or because they feel angry or resentful. Moralistic disciplinary methods, where children are seen as sinful or bad, have a devastating effect on them. Children are not inherently evil or born bad. Many parents, though they do not consciously subscribe to this belief, unconsciously believe that children are bad and tend to treat them accordingly. However, children who are fortunate in having decent, moral parents do not need to be taught moral principles; they will learn ethical behavior and decency through observing and imitating their parents. Lectures and object lessons about goodness and righteousness are often counterproductive and can be damaging, especially when parents fail to live up to their own principles.

Avoid teaching children that they are bad or selfish for wanting or having desires. Children's wants are an important part of their personal identity. They are indications of their unique interests. Pay attention to what lights your child up and appeals especially to him or her. Support these aspects of your child's personality.

While disciplining your child, it is important to stress the fact that your child's behavior is irritating or offensive, not that he or she is a bad person. Your child will know that you are not angry at him or her as a person, but at his or her behavior, which he or she can change. Afterward, reassure your child that he or she is not a bad person. You can also use humor to help your child get out of a bad mood and stop misbehaving. Humor reinforces the child's positive self-image while gently attacking the unpleasant behavior. This does not include the sarcasm or hurtful barbs that some parents use in order to control or humiliate their children; to the contrary, this style of humor is respectful of the child.

Exercise 9.3: You As a Parent: Your Critical Inner Voice/The Real You

If you hold judgmental, condemning attitudes toward yourself as a parent, it certainly interferes with your being an effective parent. It is important to separate our real perceptions of ourselves as parents from those of our critical inner voice. Exercise 9.3 will help you to separate your critical inner voices about you as a parent from your more realistic thoughts.

On the left-hand side of the page, write your critical inner voices about yourself as a parent. On the right-hand side of the page, write a more realistic view of yourself as a parent. There may be real behaviors or attitudes you exhibit that you regard as faulty: after all, no parent is perfect. But it is important to separate the realistic perception of your shortcomings from a hostile view of yourself that is punishing toward you and does not lead to your improving your behavior. If there are real behaviors or attitudes we hold as parents that we don't like in ourselves, it is important to identify them and work toward changing them so we can become the best parents we can be.

Let Your Children Love You

Our children need to be able to feel their loving feelings for us, for the people we really are behind our roles as parents. If we deny this opportunity to our children, they will suffer emotionally. We need to learn to be receptive to our children's spontaneous expressions of affection and love toward us. This seems obvious, yet it may be the most difficult task faced by us as parents. We must pay close attention to our reactions to loving expressions from our children and the feelings that these expressions arouse in us. We can then attempt to tolerate any feelings of poignant sadness and pain without pushing our children away.

We can best help our children not by sacrificing ourselves for them, but by trying to fulfill our own lives. When we are involved in an honest pursuit of our own goals, we serve as positive role models for our children. To teach our children how to live the good life, we have to genuinely value ourselves, accept all of our feelings, wants, and priorities, and actively participate in our own lives. We need to live according to our own wants and desires, from our real selves, instead of acting out the dictates of the critical inner voice. To the extent that we challenge the destructive thoughts of the inner voice and retain our capacity for feeling and a willingness to invest fully in our lives, we will have a profoundly positive effect on the personal development of our children and on their future.

There is hope in understanding how people form their defenses and how destructive thoughts are learned and transmitted from parent to child. There is much reason for optimism, because we have found that by not surrendering to the critical inner voice and its negative programming, people can break the chain of pain and defensive behaviors that is passed from generation to generation. If we continue to develop ourselves personally and strengthen our real selves, we will be better parents and our children will have a stronger sense of themselves.

Exercise 9.1: The Firestone Voice Scale for Parents

Circle the frequency with which you experience the following critical inner voices:

0 = Never   1 = Rarely   2 = Once in a while   3 = Frequently   4 = Most of the time

0 1 2 3 4   You don't know how to comfort your baby. You can't make him (her) feel better.

0 1 2 3 4   You don't know the first thing about being a parent.

0 1 2 3 4   You don't know how to handle a baby. You're going to drop it. If you don't hurt it physically, you're going to hurt it mentally.

0 1 2 3 4   You're so impatient with kids.

0 1 2 3 4   Who cares about what *you're* feeling as a parent? Your feelings aren't important. The only thing that matters is what your husband (wife) is feeling, what your child is feeling.

0 1 2 3 4   Your baby is so demanding, so needy, so clingy.

0 1 2 3 4   You've wanted a baby for years, and now you can't wait till he (she) goes to sleep. What's the matter with you?

0 1 2 3 4   Your child is supposed to fit into your life, not disrupt it.

0 1 2 3 4   Your baby is always crying. You must be doing something wrong.

0 1 2 3 4   Look, you got spanked as a kid; that's how you learned the difference between right and wrong. The only effective way to discipline children is to physically punish them. It's for their own good.

0 1 2 3 4   (Fathers) Men don't know how to take care of a baby, so let your wife do it.

0 1 2 3 4   (Mothers) Men don't know how to take care of a baby, so you should just do it all yourself.

0 1 2 3 4   You can't let kids get away with anything. You have to show them who's the boss whatever way you can.

0 1 2 3 4   You're going to spoil that child. You should just let him (her) cry himself (herself) to sleep.

0 1 2 3 4   Don't show him (her) that you are proud of him (her). You'll just make him (her) feel full of himself (herself).

0 1 2 3 4   Children are born aggressive, greedy, and selfish and have to be taught how to be civilized and unselfish.

0 1 2 3 4   You've got to clamp down early, so children won't grow up to be bad.

0 1 2 3 4   You've got to keep close tabs on your teenagers, even if it means going through their mail and personal belongings.

0 1 2 3 4   How can you even talk about being deprived as a child? You had everything, two parents, a sister, a nice house. You have only yourself to blame for the problems you're having as a parent.

0 1 2 3 4   Your children are misbehaving in public again. See how bad they're making you look!

0 1 2 3 4   That kid is just trying to get under your skin.

0 1 2 3 4   See how unhappy your child looks. It's all your fault.

0 1 2 3 4   That baby's always waking up early just to bother you.

0 1 2 3 4   You gave in to that kid again. You never do what you say you're going to do.

0 1 2 3 4   That child is rotten just like his (her) father (mother).

0 1 2 3 4   You're such an angry parent. You lose your temper all the time.

0 1 2 3 4   Your child has to learn that you mean what you say. Go ahead and spank him (her).

0 1 2 3 4   He (she) is too old for you to hug or hold him (her) all the time.

Exercise 9.2: What Do You Think When You Are Angry at Your Child?

Angry thoughts toward my child	Critical inner voices similar to the angry thoughts I have toward my child	Similar angry statements that were said to me as a child

Exercise 9.3: You as a Parent:
Your Critical Inner Voice/The Real You

My critical inner voice's point of view about me as a parent	My realistic point of view about me as a parent

Chapter 10

Living Free of Imagined Limitations—The "Good Life"

Seek not good from without: seek it within yourselves, or you will never find it.

—Epictetus

Each of us has the goal of creating the best life possible for ourselves and our loved ones. For centuries, philosophers and religious teachers have attempted to describe what it means to live the "good life." Their ideas on the subject differ, yet they all hold one belief in common—that is, that "the unexamined life is not worth living," as Socrates put it. We can fulfill our human potential only if we seriously consider our own wants, desires, goals, and ideals, and then make conscious choices as we search for personal meaning in our lives.

What Does "Living the Good Life" Mean to You?

The good life involves discovering what lies beyond your defenses and the life prescribed by your critical inner voice; it involves establishing genuinely loving relationships in spite of the interpersonal pain and suffering inherent in the human condition. The good life is not achieved by seeking to be "happy" in the sense that this word is often used—to describe an absence of unpleasant experiences such as fear, anxiety, or pain. To the contrary, to be fully alive means opening yourself up to all dimensions of life—sadness as well as joy, and pain as well as pleasure. It also involves committing yourself to a search for personal meaning and transcendent goals—of which happiness is a by-product.

There is no formula for what makes up a meaningful life for any given person. Each dimension of the good life challenges the limitations the critical inner voice has been imposing on us. Attaining the kind of life we want to live and developing our human potentialities is a lifelong project that involves dedication and a focus on what is essentially human in all of us.

It is possible to establish our goals for a better life by understanding what it truly means to be a human being. The essential human qualities in each of us include: our desire to search for meaning in life; our ability to love and to feel compassion for ourselves and others; our capacity for reasoning and creativity; our ability to experience deep emotion; our desire and need for social affiliation; our ability to set goals and develop strategies to accomplish them; our awareness of our mortality and aloneness; and our ability and desire to ponder the sacredness and mystery of life. We need to be willing to take the risks necessary to lead a self-affirming life and suffer through the accompanying anxiety. Our *life-affirming human potentialities* are those abilities that enhance life for ourselves and others. Your own way of developing these attributes is unique to your abilities and particular life situation, but it will almost certainly involve having both a desire for self-knowledge and a vision of the future.

Although it is not possible to lay out a detailed blueprint of how to attain the good life, there are several actions that you can take to move in the direction of living a more self-affirming existence. The following guidelines, used as a supplement to the techniques and exercises suggested earlier in this book, can help you further break down your defenses and overcome self-imposed barriers to your freedom.

Guidelines for Continued Personal Development

By embarking on the adventure of seeking the good life, you are giving yourself value. Because our self-image is often seriously damaged, all of us have trouble seeing ourselves as worthwhile and our lives as having intrinsic value. For this reason, freeing yourself of your early programming—separating out negative ways of thinking from a more realistic, compassionate view—becomes an important ongoing pursuit. When you can see the world through your own eyes instead of through the distorted filter of the critical inner voice, your perspective of yourself, of others, and of the world will be transformed. You will become very much like an explorer, a discoverer of your own inner world, where you uncritically investigate any thoughts or feelings you may find there.

At the same time, you will view other people and the world with real curiosity and concern. You will see people as being no different from you; you will see them as vulnerable human beings who have been damaged to a certain extent, but who may be struggling to make their lives better. You will recognize, on a deep emotional level, that ultimately we all face the same fate.

Be Aware of the Fear That Accompanies Change

It is important to emphasize again that as you move toward emotional health and a less defended life, you may experience a temporary increase in feelings of fear. It is not easy to break with your early programming and, as we have seen, there can be no growth without anxiety. It takes courage to live in a more positive environment and to take the risks necessary to be different from the identity you formed in your family.

To a certain extent, most people are afraid of change. For this reason, there are large numbers of men and women in our society who remain imprisoned to varying degrees within the armor of their defenses. They are afraid that if they give up their defenses, they will be overwhelmed by feelings of anxiety. They cannot foresee that whatever they might feel as adults could never be of the same magnitude as the feelings that overpowered them as children and originally caused them to become defended.

It is understandable that most of us have a fear of change, uncertainty, and the unfamiliar. It takes a good deal of courage to live without our customary defenses and without the critical inner voice. In fact, we must experiment and take certain risks before we know for sure how we are going to feel after we have altered our lives. Living a good life is a process; it is like a journey. It means that we gradually become accustomed to continual changes in our lives and unfamiliar landmarks in our world. After achieving a freer and more growth-enhancing life, we have to gradually become accustomed to the vast difference between this new world and the world we knew as children.

Realize That Psychological Pain Is Valid

As children, we suffered a certain amount of emotional deprivation, abuse, neglect, or indifference and, as a result, continue to suffer from psychological pain in our lives today. Many of us cover up these feelings of pain and deny to ourselves that we were treated in ways that hurt us. As a result, we begin to feel that our pain isn't valid or real, that we have no legitimate reason to be unhappy.

We may come to believe that our limitations are simply a part of us, that we were born with them, that it's just the "way we are." We may find it difficult to accept the fact that we came by them innocently and honestly—something really did happen to us that made us have to build a defensive armor that now limits our life.

Understanding that your fears have a basis and that your pain is valid is a positive step. Simply recognizing this truth can make you feel better: more in touch with your emotions and closer to yourself.

Develop a More Realistic View of Your Parents

Children are naturally lovable, yet if their parents are unable to express their love for their offspring because of their own defenses, a child often grows up feeling that he or she is somehow unlovable. When you were a child, this awareness that a parent was not capable of providing love would have left you in a hopeless situation, because your very survival was dependent on the adequacy of your parents. So children believe that they are bad and that if they change, their parents will love them. This way of thinking keeps children's hopes alive, but at a tremendous cost to themselves.

In idealizing their parents—preserving an image of them as being stronger, more positive, more loving than they actually are—children must maintain their own negative self-image. As children, we believed that the reason we were in pain was not because our parents were inadequate or weak, but because we were bad or at fault. We tend to carry this negative image with us in the form of the critical inner voice throughout life, together with feelings of being unlovable. Unless we develop a realistic picture of our parents, with their weaknesses and their strengths, we will hold on to this negative image of ourselves.

Become More Aware of Specific Defenses Against Feeling

As human beings, we have the remarkable ability to feel deeply and to reflect upon our feelings. Learning to accept all of our feelings, to understand them, and to appropriately express them is vital in maintaining emotional health. Only by leading a feelingful life can we relate to each other in a rational and peaceful manner. In contrast, it is when we are cut off from our feelings that we are the most destructive to ourselves and our loved ones.

Therefore, it is valuable to become aware of your specific defenses against feeling, whether they are self-defeating behaviors; patterns of withholding; self-denial or giving up; reliance on drugs or other substances; or a dependence on fantasies, roles, and images. Identifying the critical inner voices that influence these specific behaviors by doing the exercises in this book has probably enabled you to take control over many of them.

As you move toward living a less defended, more feelingful life, it is important to be aware that your defenses are not you. A defense that has become habitual may feel as if it is part of your identity. Understanding a defense—realizing that it is legitimate to have built that defense, yet knowing that it is now restricting you—is vital to beginning to disrupt that defense and regaining more genuine feelings for your real self.

Seek Your Own Personal Meaning in Life

As human beings, we have an intuitive feeling that there is "something more" to life than material success. We need to seek genuine personal meaning in our lives, whether through our relationships, children, work, or creative expressions. Our desire for meaning is an essential part of achieving the good life as we go beyond our more basic needs to engage in activities that we regard as having greater significance for us, for our society, and for the future. When we invest our own feelings and energy in activities that express our special wants and needs, we find that life has a unique, personal meaning for us. For example, artists find meaning in creative expression, while others find meaning in interactions with their friends and family, and others by contributing to a humanitarian cause or trying to improve conditions for future generations.

Part of our search for meaning in life involves also trying to find a balance between our work and our personal lives. It entails trying to create a home environment for ourselves and our loved ones that is optimal for the realization of each person's full potential.

Recognize the Value of Friendship

Close friendships are very different from relationships based on a fantasy bond. What distinguishes friendship from a fantasy bond is primarily the quality of the communication. There is no subject that is taboo. With a close friend you can trust, you are able to give your views and opinions and share your feelings, you are interested in your friend's perceptions of you, and you can discuss these personal opinions and perceptions without being punishing to each other. In a friendship like this, you are taking responsibility for your own anxieties and problems without making your friend a part of them. Feelings and ideas are shared with compassion for the sensitive areas in each other's life.

Such a friend can be an ally in your battle against the critical inner voice. Many people have found that meaningful contact with a close friend on an ongoing basis decreases their voice attacks and relieves their feelings of being down or depressed. It is beneficial to have a friend who possesses traits and qualities that you admire. Imitating the qualities of an admirable friend can be helpful as you continue to develop personally.

Friendship does not exist in a vacuum. It is important to share a real-life activity with your friend. This project does not have to be a huge undertaking; it can simply be appreciating a sunset together, sharing ideas, enjoying a deep interest in people. It can be any activity or interest as long as you and your friend are relating as equals. You may not be on the same level in skills, knowledge, or intelligence; however, you will feel equal because there is an absence of parent-child roles.

Guidelines for Continued Personal Development in Your Relationship

There are few experiences that make us feel more alive, that are more critical to the good life, than genuinely loving another person in the context of an intimate relationship.

In our society, the word *love* has become so trivialized that it has lost some of its real meaning. However, *love* can be meaningfully defined as feelings and behaviors that enhance the emotional well-being of oneself and the other. Loving behaviors include affection, respect for each person's boundaries, generosity, tenderness, and a desire for close companionship in life. Loving someone in our thoughts and feelings alone is not enough to create a loving relationship. We also need to express love through loving actions in order to really affect our partner in a positive way. As we stressed in chapter 4, love is a major force in life that can help dispel the pain and despair inherent in the human condition. The good life is one in which we gradually develop our capacity to offer and accept love.

As you move toward achieving the goals you have set for your relationship, it would be worthwhile to reflect on the dimensions that some couples have identified as contributing to what they considered to be an "ideal" couple interaction (Firestone and Catlett 1999). The most important factors that predicted satisfaction in a couple's interactions were the personal qualities that each partner brought to the relationship.

The qualities listed in the following section would also be important ones for people not yet in a relationship to consider when selecting a partner or potential mate. The choice of a mate has significant consequences, because the personal qualities of our partner can determine the course of our lives in many unforeseen ways. Although it is difficult to identify and evaluate positive personality traits that will endure, certain qualities can be appraised during the courtship phase. If you are not currently in a relationship, have been in an unsatisfactory one in the past, or if you are moving toward making better choices in the future, the following list can be helpful to you. The six characteristics to look for in a potential partner can also serve as ideals to strive for in further developing yourself as your relationship evolves.

Six Qualities to Look For in the "Ideal" Partner and to Develop in Yourself

This is a list of the personal qualities of the hypothetical ideal mate, as well as of qualities that you might want to further develop in yourself. These ideal qualities are contrasted with the qualities and behaviors that are typical of partners who have formed a fantasy bond (adapted from Firestone and Catlett 1999).

Positive qualities and behaviors	Qualities and behaviors typical of partners who have formed a fantasy bond
Nondefensiveness and openness	Angry reactions to feedback; closed to new experiences
Honesty and integrity	Deception and duplicity
Respect for the other's boundaries, priorities, and goals that are separate from yourself	Overstepping boundaries; other seen only in relation to yourself
Physical affection and personal sexuality	Lack of affection; inadequate or impersonal, routine sexuality
Understanding—lack of distortion of the other	Misunderstanding—distortion of the other
Noncontrolling, nonmanipulative, and nonthreatening attitudes and behaviors	Controlling, manipulative, threatening attitudes and behavior

Nondefensiveness and Openness

Two qualities essential for achieving a fulfilling relationship are openness and a lack of defensiveness. Being nondefensive means that you have developed an objective, balanced view toward yourself and your partner and that you are receptive to feedback. When men and women are being defensive in their communications, they often react with anger to criticism, no matter how mild or harsh, accurate or inaccurate the criticism is. People can intimidate their partners by changing the subject, counterattacking, breaking down and crying, or making dramatic pronouncements such as "Well, if that's the way you really think about me . . ." or "If I'm as terrible as you say I am . . . ," and so on. Needless to say, statements like these would make a person regret ever having brought up the subject. You may be defensive and overly sensitive to feedback about certain issues, while remaining open to criticism in other areas. In a marriage or a long-term relationship, partners learn quickly which subjects are "taboo" and exclude these topics from their conversations with their mates. However, this type of censorship contributes to increased tension within the relationship.

When we are nondefensive, we are also open to new experiences and take a genuine interest in learning and growing beyond our self-protective habit patterns. Men and women who are not open to the ambiguities of life tend to be inhibited and rigid. They value certainty and predictability and have routine, habitual, role-determined ways of responding to life. These couples tend to depend on familiar, conventional events such as the customary Saturday night date to give them a sense of security.

Being open allows us to take more risks, and we tend to have a strong desire to expand our boundaries and broaden our range of experiences. It is valuable to view life as an adventure and a unique opportunity to find personal meaning, instead of following prescriptions imposed on us from external sources.

Honesty and Integrity

The presence of deception is extremely damaging to a relationship. Lies and deception shatter the reality of others, eroding their belief in the truth of their perceptions. The betrayed partner ends up feeling as though he or she never really knew the other, which is a devastating feeling. In addition, when men and women are dishonest with each other and lack integrity, the communication between them gradually breaks down.

Mixed messages, where our words and actions don't match, create an atmosphere of confusion and alienation in our relationship. The greater the discrepancy between our words and our underlying feelings, the greater the potential for a disturbed relationship.

People who are honest and reliable represent themselves accurately to others as well as to themselves. In order to achieve this level of integrity, we must take the trouble to know ourselves. Having a willingness to face parts of our personality that may be unpleasant allows us to gradually modify ourselves in a positive direction.

Respect for the Other's Boundaries, Goals, and Interests

In a relationship that is truly loving, each partner respects the boundaries, interests, and aspirations of the other. Self-reliant, independent men and women show, through their words and actions, a genuine respect for the goals and priorities of their mates, even when they do not share these goals or interests.

People who have not emancipated themselves from early emotional dependency on their family often expect more security from their intimate relationships and marriage than it is possible to extract. They tend to have unrealistic hopes that all their needs will be met in a marital relationship. The burden that this anticipation puts on the relationship is tremendous; it is clear that no one person can fulfill such unrealistic expectations. In relationships characterized by a fantasy bond, each partner usually feels a sense of obligation in relation to fulfilling the other's expectations. Only when we are centered in ourselves, have a sense of self-worth, and are truly individualistic do we tend to sustain healthy relationships in which our personal freedom and that of our partner are accorded the highest priority.

Physical Affection and Sexuality

In a healthy relationship, affection and sexual relating are spontaneous and the partners are close emotionally. Both partners view sexual relating as a fulfilling aspect of life, a gift and a positive offering of pleasure to their mate and to themselves. They have mature attitudes toward sexuality and do not see it as an isolated activity separate from the rest of their lives. The way people feel about themselves as men and women, the feelings they have about their bodies, and their attitudes toward sex can enhance their sense of self and feelings of happiness.

In a relationship characterized by a fantasy bond, affectionate sexuality may degenerate into routine, habitual love-making that is impersonal or mechanical. One or both partners may be using the sexual contact to relieve anxiety or to boost self-esteem. Or a couple's sexual relating might diminish in frequency, become sporadic, or cease altogether. In both cases, the partners miss out on experiencing the part of their relationship that can be the most gratifying. This deterioration usually occurs because we seem to be the least tolerant of love in our most intimate relationships, where there is a unique opportunity for both an affectionate, feelingful exchange and a sexual response. We tend to pull back in one area or the other, avoiding the special combination of love, sexuality, and tenderness that is the most rewarding.

Empathy and Understanding

In a relationship where partners have formed a fantasy bond, there is a lack of empathy and understanding. When people don't feel listened to, taken seriously, or understood by their mates, they suffer from hurt feelings and have angry reactions. Each partner may be distorting the other based on views promoted by his or her critical inner voice. Often partners use their negative perceptions and distortions of the other to feel misunderstood. In these instances, they may be telling themselves, *"He (she) just doesn't understand you. Nobody understands you."* These distortions, which lead to diminished empathy and understanding, have a negative effect on a couple's interactions and the overall relationship.

Understanding involves seeing your partner's strengths and weaknesses without exaggerating his or her positive or negative traits and behaviors. It means valuing the commonalities as well as the differences between you and your loved one. Nothing feels as good as knowing that you are being seen for who you are; true intimacy between two people involves each developing a deep understanding of the other person. To facilitate understanding in your relationship, you would try to maintain an ongoing dialogue about your differences as well as your similarities. Empathy is an outgrowth of this type of understanding, in which a partner is able to experience how the other feels in a situation.

Nonthreatening and Nonmanipulative Behavior

Learn how to directly express your wants and desires in your relationship rather than resorting to indirect means (that is, manipulations) that make your partner feel guilty or angry. In relationships that have deteriorated into a fantasy bond, partners may use a variety of techniques to try to "keep each other in line." They nag, complain, badger, or intimidate each other into giving them what they want, but the satisfaction they receive when their manipulations are successful is hollow and often short-lived.

Some people intimidate their mates by being domineering and bossy. They overpower their partners with verbal abuse, threats of physical violence, or threats to leave if they don't get their way. Others are overly dependent and act out immature behaviors. They manipulate their partners by breaking down emotionally, giving them "the silent treatment," or threatening self-destructive actions. The absence of manipulation or threat in a relationship helps maintain the good feelings between the partners, which in turn contributes to building trust and feelings of security in the relationship.

Exercise 10.1: Ideal Qualities Checklist for Partners

Where do you see yourself and your partner on the continuum between these ideal qualities and undesirable traits and behaviors influenced by the critical inner voice? Make two copies of exercise 10.1. Complete one copy and ask your partner if he or she would like to complete the second form.

Talking About the Checklist with Your Partner

After you and your partner have completed exercise 10.1, ask whether he or she would be interested in comparing the numbers you each circled on the scale. You can begin the conversation by talking about one of the dimensions you checked off that indicates a behavior (weakness or shortcoming) you may wish to improve. Then ask for your partner's ideas or comments on this issue. When he or she is speaking, try to listen and take in any helpful feedback without reacting immediately. Give yourself a few moments to digest the information. It is important to remember that it is coming from a person who knows you well and who has a friendly point of view toward you. The resulting conversation or discussion may elicit feelings in both of you regarding your strengths as well as your shortcomings.

Guidelines for Further Developing a Meaningful Life

In addition to developing the most fulfilling relationship possible, what else can we do to enhance the meaning of our lives? Being generous in all our interactions with others is a sound mental health principle that helps us develop a good feeling about ourselves. Learning to focus on the spiritual aspects of life adds a sense of meaning to our existence. And perhaps most important, being aware of the existential realities that we all face allows us to have a deep sense of compassion for others and for ourselves.

Practice Being Generous in All Your Relationships

Generosity refers to behaviors that are outward expressions of our feelings of empathy and compassion toward family members, friends, and other fellow human beings. Generous actions ideally involve benevolent feelings on the giver's side and an openness to accepting the offering on the part of the recipient.

A person can counteract self-critical attitudes and cynical views of others through acts of generosity. When we have an opportunity to extend ourselves to others through sensitive acts of kindness and generosity, we are countering the dictates of the critical inner voice that warn us to hold back our natural tendencies to be kind or generous. Giving freely of ourselves and of our time goes against these defenses, increases our feelings of self-esteem, and makes us feel worthwhile. This process is circular: as we come to value ourselves more and cherish our experience, we naturally feel motivated to extend this same valuing and appreciation to others by being generous. Being able to act on the desire to contribute to the well-being of others brings us pleasure and gives life a special meaning.

Being generous frees up energy. When we overcome any attitudes of tightness we have, we will become more dynamic and productive in other areas of our lives. The spirit of generosity is contagious; it spreads to other people, who then discover for themselves that giving generates a sense of well-being and happiness. When our generous acts are an expression of our feelings of compassion for other people and part of an empathic response to meeting their needs, we experience a profound sense of pleasure. As we become more sensitive to others, we will begin to consider their well-being and put those feelings above our own impulse to hold back or withdraw.

Learning to accept generosity and kindness from others is as important as learning how to be generous. When people are giving to you, the attacks of the critical inner voice become strongest. Accepting something from another person threatens the self-nourishing aspect of the fantasy bond. Therefore, accepting what is offered you is crucial to breaking this defense. The positive responses of appreciation we express to a person who has been kind or generous to us are generous acts in themselves.

Develop a Spiritual Perspective and Appreciate the Mystery of Existence

As humans, we possess the ability to have spiritual experiences—that is, to go beyond the satisfaction of our material needs and sense mysteries that elude human understanding. At many points on the journey through life, people encounter events that bring out a deep appreciation of nature and the unknown and that generate spiritual experiences that evoke deep emotional responses. It is when this search for meaning and spiritual awareness takes us to the edge of human understanding—where we accept the ultimate mystery of our lives and the limitations of science and rationality—that we know at the most profound level what it means to be fully human.

In accepting the uncertainty and ambiguity of life, we can come to understand that there are no absolute "truths" to be discovered. We would know that wherever there is an absence of fact, we have the right to choose and embrace beliefs about the origins and nature of life. We would develop our own beliefs rather than accepting, without reflection, preconceived religious dogma or other belief systems.

Becoming Aware of Existential Realities

Facing the fact of our own mortality can give our lives a poignant meaning. If we imagine the end of life while we are in a less defended, more vulnerable state, we will be aware of the preciousness of each moment, and we will be likely to invest more of ourselves in our relationships. Being aware of death and facing our sadness and fears can inspire us to greater creativity and make us more compassionate toward other people.

An emotionally healthy person, one who has a minimum of defenses, has a strong investment in living and responds with appropriate feeling to both good and bad events in life. When we base our emotional reactions on real events and circumstances, rather than listening to the critical inner voice and remaining defended, we are leaving ourselves open to painful feelings. For example, on September 11, 2001, most of us turned on the morning news and within the first few seconds were bombarded with the following stories:

- Terrorist Planes Destroy World Trade Center: Thousands Feared Dead

- Suicide Plane Strikes Pentagon: Death Toll Unknown

- President Says Terrorist Attacks Are Acts of War

How do we, as feeling people, alive to all the realities of life, react to these events?

Defenses seem almost necessary when we are faced with people's inhumanity to other people. Yet cruelty, injustice, terrorism, and ethnic warfare are a result of dishonest and defended patterns of thinking and living that take away people's natural compassion for themselves and their fellow human beings.

Many people mistakenly believe that personal development should make them less sensitive to the pain of everyday living and more immune to distress from events such as these. They imagine they will be less vulnerable to hurt from failure, rejection, or loss. The opposite is true. Emotionally healthy people are acutely sensitive to events in their lives that have a negative impact on their sense of well-being or that adversely affect the people closest to them. In fact, they appear to be more responsive, not less, to emotionally painful situations than they were before they gave up many of their defenses.

On the other hand, when we are less defended, we are better able to deal with anxiety and stress and are far less susceptible to negative thinking, depression, and other symptoms of emotional disturbance. The more open we are to our emotions, the more we can tolerate irrational, angry, competitive, or other "unacceptable" feelings in ourselves. Because of this, we are less compelled to act out these feelings in interactions with our friends and family members.

In contrast, people who remain defended and cut off from their feelings often have melodramatic reactions to minor personal slights or imagined rejections, yet they may lack feeling in response to real hardship or adversity. They seem to be one step removed from directly experiencing the world around them and have conventional or role-determined reactions to important events in life. Their defenses act to suppress their genuine feelings. As a result, their reactions are more automatic, impersonal, or intellectual.

It seems that living with the poignant awareness of existential issues is too agonizing for many people to endure. Consequently, many of us slowly commit emotional suicide. The critical inner voice plays a central role in influencing us to gradually give up our active involvement in life. Just as it encourages us to protect ourselves against future rejection in our personal relationships by holding back our love, it persuades us to hold back our emotional involvement in life itself to gain an imaginary sense of control over death.

The dilemma involved in being more aware of painful aspects of the human condition and the reality of death presents us with a choice between putting our defensive armor back on or living without its protection. We *could* choose to face death straightforwardly and feel sad about the future loss of ourselves and our loved ones. Understanding that all people ultimately share the same fate would allow us to view our fellow human beings with more compassion and understanding. We would see no person as inferior or superior to us, nor would we invest any person with greater or lesser status. Being aware of our limitation in time would make life and living all the more precious.

Exercise 10.1: Ideal Qualities Checklist for Partners

How much of the time do you and your partner display these qualities?

0 = Never   1 = Rarely   2 = Once in a while   3 = Frequently   4 = Most of the time

Me   Partner

0 1 2 3 4   0 1 2 3 4   Nondefensive and open (able to listen to feedback without overreacting; open to new experiences)

0 1 2 3 4   0 1 2 3 4   Has respect for the other's boundaries (valuing the desires and priorities of the other separate from your own self-interest)

0 1 2 3 4   0 1 2 3 4   Vulnerable (willing to feel sad, acknowledge hurt feelings, etc.)

0 1 2 3 4   0 1 2 3 4   Honest (straightforward, nondeceptive, actions match your words)

0 1 2 3 4   0 1 2 3 4   Physically affectionate

0 1 2 3 4   0 1 2 3 4   Sexual (satisfied with sexual relationship)

0 1 2 3 4   0 1 2 3 4   Empathic and understanding (lack of distortion of the other, valuing differences as well as commonalities)

0 1 2 3 4   0 1 2 3 4   Communicative (sense of shared meaning; feel understood)

0 1 2 3 4   0 1 2 3 4   Noncontrolling (nonmanipulative and nonthreatening)

How would you rate yourself along these dimensions?

0 1 2 3 4   Sense of well-being

0 1 2 3 4   Self-confidence

0 1 2 3 4   Optimism

Bibliography

Doucette-Gates, A., R. W. Firestone, and L. Firestone. 1999. Assessing Violent Thoughts: The Relationship between Thought Processes and Violent Behavior. *Psychologica Belgica* 39:113–134.

Firestone, L., and J. Catlett. 1998. The Treatment of Sylvia Plath. *Death Studies* 22:667–692

Firestone, R. W. 1984. A Concept of the Primary Fantasy Bond: A Developmental Perspective. *Psychotherapy* 21:218–225.

———. 1985. *The Fantasy Bond: Structure of Psychological Defenses*. Santa Barbara, CA: Glendon Association.

———. 1986. The "Inner Voice" and Suicide. *Psychotherapy* 23:439–447.

———. 1987. Destructive Effects of the Fantasy Bond in Couple and Family Relationships. *Psychotherapy* 24:233–239.

———. 1987. The "Voice": The Dual Nature of Guilt Reactions. *American Journal of Psychoanalysis* 47:210–229.

———. 1988. *Voice Therapy: A Psychotherapeutic Approach to Self-Destructive Behavior*. Santa Barbara, Calif.: Glendon Association.

———. 1989. Parenting Groups Based on Voice Therapy. *Psychotherapy* 26:524–529.

————. 1990. The Bipolar Causality of Regression. *American Journal of Psychoanalysis* 50:121–135.

————. 1990. *Compassionate Child-Rearing: An In-Depth Approach to Optimal Parenting*. Santa Barbara, Calif.: Glendon Association.

————. 1990. Prescription for Psychotherapy. *Psychotherapy* 27:627–635

————. 1990. Voice Therapy. In *What Is Psychotherapy? Contemporary Perspectives*, edited by J. Zeig and W. Munion. San Francisco: Jossey-Bass.

————. 1990. Voices During Sex: Application of Voice Therapy to Sexuality. *Journal of Sex and Marital Therapy* 16:258–274.

————. 1993. The Psychodynamics of Fantasy, Addiction, and Addictive Attachments. *American Journal of Psychoanalysis* 53:335–352.

————. 1994. A New Perspective on the Oedipal Complex: A Voice Therapy Session. *Psychotherapy* 31:342–351.

————. 1994. Psychological Defenses against Death Anxiety. In *Death Anxiety Handbook: Research, Instrumentation, and Application*, edited by R. A. Neimeyer. Washington, D.C.: Taylor & Francis.

————. 1996. The Origins of Ethnic Strife. *Mind and Human Interaction* 7:167–180.

————. 1997. *Combating Destructive Thought Processes: Voice Therapy and Separation Theory*. Thousand Oaks, Calif.: Sage.

————. 1997. *Suicide and the Inner Voice: Risk Assessment, Treatment, and Case Management*. Thousand Oaks, Calif.: Sage.

————. 1998. Voice Therapy. In *Favorite Counseling and Therapy Techniques: 51 Therapists Share Their Most Creative Strategies*, edited by H. G. Rosenthal. Washington, D.C.: Accelerated Development.

————. 2000. Microsuicide and the Elderly: A Basic Defense against Death Anxiety. In *Death Attitudes and the Older Adult: Theories, Concepts, and Applications*, edited by A. Tomer. Philadelphia: Brunner-Routledge.

————. 2001. Behavioral Assignments for Individual and Couples Therapy: Corrective Suggestions for Behavioral Change. In *Favorite Counseling and Therapy Homework Assignments: Leading Therapists Share Their Most Creative Strategies*, edited by H. G. Rosenthal. Philadelphia: Brunner-Routledge.

Firestone, R. W., and J. Catlett. 1989. *Psychological Defenses in Everyday Life*. Santa Barbara, Calif.: Glendon Association.

————. 1999. *Fear of Intimacy*. Washington, D.C.: American Psychological Association.

————. In press. *The Good Life: Sustaining Feeling in a High-Tech Age*. Washington, D.C.: American Psychological Association.

Firestone, R. W., and L. Firestone. 1996. *Firestone Assessment of Self-Destructive Thoughts*. San Antonio, Tex.: Psychological Corporation.

————. 1998. Voices in Suicide: The Relationship between Self-Destructive Thought Processes, Maladaptive Behavior, and Self-Destructive Manifestations. *Death Studies* 22:411–443.

————. In press. Suicide Reduction and Prevention. In *The Benefits of Counselling and Psychotherapy*, edited by C. Feltham. London: Sage Publications.

Firestone, R. W., and R. H. Seiden. 1987. Microsuicide and Suicidal Threats of Everyday Life. *Psychotherapy* 24:31–39.

————. 1990. Psychodynamics in Adolescent Suicide. *Journal of College Student Psychotherapy* 4:101–123.

————. 1990. Suicide and the Continuum of Self-Destructive Behavior. *Journal of American College Health* 38:207–213.

Glendon Association Video Productions

Fantasy Bond

Parr, G., producer. 1985. *The Fantasy Bond*. Santa Barbara, Calif.: Glendon Association. Videocassette.

Parent/Child Relations

Parr, G., producer. 1984. *Teaching Our Children about Feelings*. Santa Barbara, Calif.: Glendon Association. Videocassette.

————. 1986. *The Inner Voice in Child Abuse*. Santa Barbara, Calif.: Glendon Association. Videocassette.

————. 1987. *Hunger Versus Love*. Santa Barbara, Calif.: Glendon Association. Videocassette.

————. 1987. *Therapeutic Child-Rearing*. Santa Barbara, Calif.: Glendon Association. Videocassette.

————. 1987. *Parental Ambivalence*. Santa Barbara, Calif.: Glendon Association. Videocassette.

————. 1988. *The Implicit Pain of Sensitive Child-Rearing*. Santa Barbara, Calif.: Glendon Association. Videocassette.

————. 1994. *Invisible Child Abuse*. Santa Barbara, Calif.: Glendon Association. Videocassette.

Couple Relations

Parr, G., producer. 1986. *Closeness Without Bonds*. Santa Barbara, Calif.: Glendon Association. Videocassette.

———. 1989. *Bobby and Rosie: Anatomy of a Marriage*. Santa Barbara, Calif.: Glendon Association. Videocassette.

———. 1990. *Sex and Marriage*. Santa Barbara, Calif.: Glendon Association. Videocassette.

———. 1990. *Sex and Society*. Santa Barbara, Calif.: Glendon Association. Videocassette.

———. 1990. *Voices in Sex*. Santa Barbara, Calif.: Glendon Association. Videocassette.

———. 1995. *Voices about Relationships*. Santa Barbara, Calif.: Glendon Association. Videocassette.

———. 1997. *Exploring Relationships*. Santa Barbara, Calif.: Glendon Association. Videocassette.

———. 1997. *Fear of Intimacy*. Santa Barbara, Calif.: Glendon Association. Videocassette.

———. 1999. *Coping with the Fear of Intimacy*. Santa Barbara, Calif.: Glendon Association. Videocassette.

Friendship/Adventure Series

Parr, G., producer. 1983. *Voyage to Understanding*. Santa Barbara, Calif.: Glendon Association. Videocassette.

———. 1993. *Children of the Summer*. Santa Barbara, Calif.: Glendon Association. Videocassette.

Business Relations

Parr, G., producer. 1989. *Of Business and Friendship*. Santa Barbara, Calif.: Glendon Association. Videocassette.

Existential Issues

Parr, G., producer. 1990. *Life, Death, and Denial*. Santa Barbara, Calif.: Glendon Association. Videocassette.

———. 1990. *Defenses against Death Anxiety*. Santa Barbara, Calif.: Glendon Association. Videocassette.

Glendon Association Web site
   www.glendon.org

Suggested Reading

Chapter 1

Bach, G., and L. Torbet. 1983. *The Inner Enemy: How to Fight Fair with Yourself.* New York: William Morrow.

Epstein, S. 1998. *Constructive Thinking: The Key to Emotional Intelligence.* Westport, Conn.: Praeger Publishers.

Forward, S., with C. Buck. 1989. *Toxic Parents: Overcoming Their Hurtful Legacy and Reclaiming Your Life.* New York: Bantam Books.

Gootnick, I. 1997. *Why You Behave in Ways You Hate: And What You Can Do about It.* Granite Bay, Calif.: Penmarin Books.

Grudermeyer, D., R. Grudermeyer, and L. N. Patrick. 1996. *Sensible Self-Help: The First Road Map for the Healing Journey.* Del Mar, Calif.: Willingness Works Press.

Halpern, H. M. 1976. *Cutting Loose: An Adult's Guide to Coming to Terms with Your Parents.* New York: Simon & Schuster.

Loring, M. T. 1994. *Emotional Abuse: The Trauma and the Treatment.* San Francisco: Jossey-Bass.

Love, P., with J. Robinson. 1990. *The Emotional Incest Syndrome: What to Do When a Parent's Love Rules Your Life.* New York: Bantam Books.

Matsakis, A. 1998. *Trust after Trauma: A Guide to Relationships for Survivors and Those Who Love Them.* Oakland, Calif.: New Harbinger Publications.

McKay, M., M. Davis, and P. Fanning. 1997. *Thoughts and Feelings: Taking Control of Your Moods and Your Life.* Oakland, Calif.: New Harbinger Publications.

McKay, M., and P. Fanning. 1991. *Prisoners of Belief.* Oakland, Calif.: New Harbinger Publications.

Chapter 2

Dillon, S., with M. C. Benson. 2001. *The Woman's Guide to Total Self-Esteem: The Eight Secrets You Need to Know.* Oakland, Calif.: New Harbinger Publications.

Lewis, M. 1992. *Shame: The Exposed Self.* New York: Free Press.

Matsakis, A. 1999. *Survivor Guilt: A Self-Help Guide.* Oakland, Calif.: New Harbinger Publications.

McKay, M., and P. Fanning. 2000. *Self-Esteem*, 3d ed. Oakland, Calif.: New Harbinger Publications.

McKay, M., P. Fanning, C. Honeychurch, and C. Sutker. 1999. *The Self-Esteem Companion.* Oakland, Calif.: New Harbinger Publications.

Potter-Efron, R., and P. Potter-Efron. 1999. *The Secret Message of Shame: Pathways to Hope and Healing.* Oakland, Calif.: New Harbinger Publications.

Rubin, T. E., with E. Rubin. 1975. *Compassion and Self-Hate: An Alternative to Despair.* New York: David McKay.

Rutledge, T. 1997. *The Self-Forgiveness Handbook: A Practical and Empowering Guide.* Oakland, Calif.: New Harbinger Publications.

———. 1998. *Earning Your Own Respect: A Handbook of Personal Responsibility.* Oakland, Calif.: New Harbinger Publications.

Chapter 3

Bardwick, J. M. 1991. *Danger in the Comfort Zone: From Boardroom to Mailroom— How to Break the Entitlement Habit That's Killing American Business.* New York: American Management Association.

Blanchard, K., and S. Johnson. 1981. *The One Minute Manager: The Quickest Way to Increase Your Own Prosperity.* New York: Berkley Books.

Canfield, J., M. V. Hansen, and L. Hewitt. 2000. *The Power of Focus.* Deerfield Beach, Fla.: Health Communications.

Carnegie, D. 1998. *Dale Carnegie's Lifetime Plan for Success: How to Win Friends and Influence People: How to Stop Worrying and Start Living.* New York: Galahad Books.

Covey, S. R., A. R. Merrill, and R. R. Merrill. 1994. *First Things First: To Live, to Love, to Learn, to Leave a Legacy.* New York: Simon & Schuster.

Dickson, A. 2000. *Women at Work: Strategies for Survival and Success.* London: Kogan Page.

DuBrin, A. J. 1992. *Your Own Worst Enemy: How to Overcome Career Self-Sabotage.* New York: American Management Association.

Gallwey, W. T. 2000. *The Inner Game of Work: Focus, Learning, Pleasure, and Mobility in the Workplace.* New York: Random House.

Goldratt, E. M., and J. Cox. 1992. *The Goal: A Process of Ongoing Improvement.* Great Barrington, Mass.: North River Press Publishing.

Maxwell, J. C. 2000. *Failing Forward: Turning Mistakes into Stepping-Stones for Success.* Nashville, Tenn.: Thomas Nelson.

Myerson, M. 1999. *Six Keys to Creating the Life You Desire: Stop Pursuing the Unattainable and Find the Fulfillment You Truly Need.* Oakland, Calif.: New Harbinger Publications.

Peters, T. J., and R. H. Waterman, Jr. 1982. *In Search of Excellence: Lessons from America's Best-Run Companies.* New York: Warner Books.

Roberts, M. S. 1995. *Living Without Procrastination.* Oakland, Calif.: New Harbinger Publications.

Soundview Editorial Staff, eds. 1989. *Skills for Success: The Experts Show the Way.* Bristol, Vt.: Soundview Executive Book Summaries.

Tichy, N. M., and S. Sherman. 1993. *Control Your Destiny or Someone Else Will: How Jack Welch Is Making General Electric the World's Most Competitive Corporation.* New York: Doubleday.

Zimmerman, F. 2001. *Reinvent Your Work: How to Rejuvenate, Revamp, or Recreate Your Career.* Chicago: Dearborn Trade Publishing.

Chapter 4

Bach, G. R., and R. M. Deutsch. 1979. *Stop! You're Driving Me Crazy: How to Keep the People in Your Life from Driving You up the Wall.* New York: Berkley Books.

Bader, E., and P. T. Pearson, with J. D. Schwartz. 2000. *Tell Me No Lies: How to Face the Truth and Build a Loving Marriage.* New York: St. Martin's Press.

Beck, A. T. 1988. *Love Is Never Enough.* New York: Harper & Row.

Gottman, J., with N. Silver. 1994. *Why Marriages Succeed or Fail: And How You Can Make Yours Last.* New York: Simon & Schuster.

Gottman J. M., and N. Silver. 1999. *Seven Principles for Making a Marriage Work*. New York: Three Rivers Press.

Hendrix, H., and H. Hunt. 1994. *The Couple's Companion: Meditations and Exercises for Getting the Love You Want*. New York: Pocket Books.

Lassen, M. 2000. *Why Are We Still Fighting? How to End Your Schema Wars and Start Connecting with the People You Love*. Oakland, Calif.: New Harbinger Publications.

Lerner, H. 1989. *The Dance of Intimacy: A Woman's Guide to Courageous Acts of Change in Key Relationships*. New York: HarperPerennial.

———. 1985. *The Dance of Anger: A Woman's Guide to Changing the Patterns of Intimate Relationships*. New York: Harper & Row.

Love, P. 2001. *The Truth About Love: The Highs, the Lows, and How You Can Make It Last Forever*. New York: Simon & Schuster.

Lyons, M., and J. Psaris. 2000. *Undefended Love*. Oakland, Calif.: New Harbinger Publications.

Markman, H. J., S. M. Stanley, and S. L. Blumberg. 2001. *Fighting for Your Marriage: Positive Steps for Preventing Divorce and Preserving a Lasting Love*, rev. ed. San Francisco: Jossey-Bass.

McKay, M., P. Fanning, and K. Paleg. 1994. *Couple Skills: Making Your Relationship Work*. Oakland, Calif.: New Harbinger Publications.

Mellody, P., with A. W. Miller and J. K. Miller. 1992. *Facing Love Addiction: Giving Yourself the Power to Change the Way You Love—The Love Connection to Codependence*. San Francisco: HarperCollins.

Pietsch, W. V. 2000. *Human BE-ing: How to Have a Creative Relationship Instead of a Power Struggle*. Victoria, B.C., Canada: Trafford Publishing.

Wallerstein, J. S., and S. Blakeslee. 1995. *The Good Marriage: How and Why Love Lasts*. Boston: Houghton Mifflin.

Chapter 5

Beaver, D. 1992. *More Than Just Sex: A Committed Couple's Guide to Keeping Relationships Lively, Intimate, and Gratifying*. Fairfield, Conn.: Aslan Publishing.

Calderone, M. S., and E. W. Johnson. 1989. *The Family Book about Sexuality*, rev. ed. New York: Harper & Row.

Carnes, P. 1997. *Sexual Anorexia: Overcoming Sexual Self-Hatred*. Center City, Minn.: Hazelden.

Comfort, A. 1991. *The New Joy of Sex: A Gourmet Guide to Lovemaking for the Nineties*. New York: Pocket Books.

Ellenberg, D., and J. Bell. 1995. *Lovers for Life: Creating Lasting Passion, Trust, and True Partnership*. Santa Rosa, Calif.: Aslan Publishing.

Ellison, C. 2000. *Women's Sexualities: Generations of Women Share Intimate Secrets of Sexual Self-Acceptance*. Oakland, Calif.: New Harbinger Publications.

Schnarch, D. 1997. *Passionate Marriage: Love, Sex, and Intimacy in Emotionally Committed Relationships*. New York: Henry Holt.

Zoldbrod, A. 1998. *Sex Smart: How Your Childhood Shaped Your Sexual Life and What to Do about It*. Oakland, Calif.: New Harbinger Publications.

Chapter 6

Daley, D. C. 1991. *Kicking Addictive Habits Once and for All: A Relapse Prevention Guide*. San Francisco: Jossey-Bass.

Fanning, P., and J. O'Neill. 1996. *The Addiction Workbook: A Step-by-Step Guide to Quitting Alcohol and Drugs*. Oakland, Calif.: New Harbinger Publications.

Greenfield, D. N. 1999. *Virtual Addiction: Help for Netheads, Cyberfreaks, and Those Who Love Them*. Oakland, Calif.: New Harbinger Publications.

Hall, L., and L. Cohn. 1990. *Self-Esteem: Tools for Recovery*. Carlsbad, Calif.: Gurze Books.

Nakken, C. 1988. *The Addictive Personality: Understanding the Addictive Process and Compulsive Behavior*. Center City, Minn.: Hazelden.

Pardee, P. 1998. *A Voice of Hope: A Workbook for Adults Recovering from Chemical Dependency*. Soquel, Calif.: ToucanEd Publications.

Sandbek, T. J. 1993. *The Deadly Diet*, 2d ed. Oakland, Calif.: New Harbinger Publications.

Santoro, J., A. Bergman, and R. DeLetis. 2001. *Kill The Craving*. Oakland, Calif.: New Harbinger Publications.

Schwartz, J. M., with B. Beyette. 1996. *Brain Lock: Free Yourself from Obsessive-Compulsive Behavior*. New York: ReganBooks.

Seixas, J. S., and G. Youcha. 1985. *Children of Alcoholism: A Survivor's Manual*. New York: Harper & Row.

Siegel, M., J. Brisman, and M. Weinshel. 1997. *Surviving an Eating Disorder: Strategies for Family and Friends*, rev. ed. New York: HarperPerennial.

Washton, A., and D. Boundy. 1989. *Willpower's Not Enough: Understanding and Recovering from Addictions of Every Kind*. New York: HarperPerennial.

Chapter 7

Burns, D. 1980. *Feeling Good: The New Mood Therapy*. New York: William Morrow.

Carlson, T. 1998. *Depression in the Young: What We Can Do to Help Them*. Duluth, Minn.: Benline Press.

Copeland, M. E. 1992. *The Depression Workbook: A Guide for Living with Depression*. Oakland, Calif.: New Harbinger Publications.

———. 1994. *Coping with Depression*. Oakland, Calif.: New Harbinger Publications.

Cronkite, K. 1994. *On the Edge of Darkness: Conversations about Conquering Depression*. New York: Delta.

Ellis, T. E., and C. F. Newman. 1996. *Choosing to Live: How to Defeat Suicide Through Cognitive Therapy*. Oakland, Calif.: New Harbinger Publications.

Fieve, R. R. 1989. *Moodswing*, rev. ed. New York: William Morrow.

Gordon, S. 1985. *When Living Hurts*. New York: Dell.

Gottlieb, M. M. 1999. *The Angry Self: A Comprehensive Approach to Anger Management*. Phoenix: Zeig, Tucker & Co.

Greenberger, D., and C. A. Padesky. 1995. *Mind Over Mood: Change How You Feel by Changing the Way You Think*. New York: Guilford Press.

Jamison, K. R. 1999. *Night Falls Fast: Understanding Suicide*. New York: Alfred A. Knopf.

Preston, J. 2001. *Lift Your Mood Now*. Oakland, Calif.: New Harbinger Publications.

Chapter 8

Beutler, L. E., B. Bongar, and J. N. Shurkin. 1998. *Am I Crazy, or Is It My Shrink?* New York: Oxford University Press.

Chapter 9

Adams, C., and E. Fruge 1996. *Why Children Misbehave and What to Do about It*. Oakland, Calif.: New Harbinger Publications.

Becnel, B. C. 1991. *The Co-Dependent Parent: Free Yourself by Freeing Your Child*. San Francisco: HarperCollins.

Brazelton, T. B. 1987. *What Every Baby Knows*. New York: Ballantine Books.

Brazelton, T. B., and B. G. Cramer. 1990. *The Earliest Relationship: Parents, Infants, and the Drama of Early Attachment*. Reading, Mass.: Addison-Wesley.

Brazelton, T. B., and S. I. Greenspan. 2000. *The Irreducible Needs of Children: What Every Child Must Have to Grow, Learn, and Flourish*. Cambridge, Mass.: Perseus Publishing.

Brown, N. 2001. *Children of the Self-Absorbed: A Grownup's Guide to Getting Over Narcissistic Parents.* Oakland, Calif.: New Harbinger Publications.

Elliott, C. H., and L. L. Smith. 1999. *Why Can't I Be the Parent I Want to Be?: End Old Patterns and Enjoy Your Children.* Oakland, Calif.: New Harbinger Publications.

Fraiberg, S. H. 1959. *The Magic Years: Understanding and Handling the Problems of Early Childhood.* New York: Charles Scribner's Sons.

Haffner, D. W. 1999. *From Diapers to Dating: A Parent's Guide to Raising Sexually Healthy Children.* New York: Newmarket Press.

Johnson, T. C. 1999. *Understanding Your Child's Sexual Behavior: What's Natural and Healthy.* Oakland, Calif.: New Harbinger Publications.

Kendall-Tackett, K. A. 2001. *The Hidden Feelings of Motherhood: Coping with Stress, Depression, and Burnout.* Oakland, Calif.: New Harbinger Publications.

McKay, M., K. Paleg, P. Fanning, and D. Landis. 1996. *When Anger Hurts Your Kids: A Parent's Guide.* Oakland, Calif.: New Harbinger Publications.

Paleg, K. 1997. *The Ten Things Every Parent Needs to Know.* Oakland, Calif.: New Harbinger Publications.

Pope, A. W., S. M. McHale, and W. E. Craighead. 1988. *Self-Esteem Enhancement with Children and Adolescents.* New York: Pergamon Press.

Scott Newman Center. 1991. *Straight Talk with Kids: Improving Communication, Building Trust, and Keeping Your Children Drug Free.* New York: Bantam Books.

Skynner, R., and J. Cleese. 1983. *Families and How to Survive Them.* New York: Oxford University Press.

Winnicott, D. W. 1993. *Talking to Parents.* Reading, Mass.: Addison-Wesley.

Witkin, G. 1999. *Kid Stress: What It Is, How It Feels, How to Help.* New York: Penguin Books.

Chapter 10

Charnetski, C. J., and F. X. Brennan. 2001. *Feeling Good Is Good for You: How Pleasure Can Boost Your Immune System and Lengthen Your Life.* Emmaus, Penn.: Rodale Press.

Covey, S. R. 1999. *Living the 7 Habits: The Courage to Change.* New York: Simon & Schuster.

The Dalai Lama. 2000. *Transforming the Mind: Teachings on Generating Compassion.* Translated by G. T. Jinpa. London: Thorsons.

Frankl, V. E. 1984. *Man's Search for Meaning: An Introduction to Logotherapy*, 3d ed. New York: Simon & Schuster.

Fromm, E. 1956. *The Art of Loving*. New York: Bantam Books.

Jenson, J. C. 1995. *Reclaiming Your Life: A Step-by-Step Guide to Using Regression Therapy to Overcome the Effects of Childhood Abuse*. New York: Meridian.

Kaufman, G., and L. Raphael. 1983. *Dynamics of Power: Building a Competent Self*. Cambridge, Mass.: Schenkman Books.

Laing, R. D. 1967. *The Politics of Experience*. New York: Ballantine Books.

Levine, S. 1997. *A Year to Live: How to Live This Year as if It Were Your Last*. New York: Bell Tower.

Meyerson, M., and L. Ashner. 1999. *Six Keys to Creating the Life You Desire*. Oakland, Calif.: New Harbinger Publications.

Miller, A. 1993. *Breaking Down the Wall of Silence: The Liberating Experience of Facing Painful Truth*. Translated by S. Worrall. New York: Meridian.

———. 2001. *The Truth Will Set You Free: Overcoming Emotional Blindness and Finding Your True Adult Self*. New York: Basic Books.

Pelzer, D. 2000. *Help Yourself: Finding Hope, Courage, and Happiness*. New York: Plume.

Sheehy, G. 1995. *New Passages: Mapping Your Life across Time*. New York: Ballantine Books.

Tart, C. T. 1994. *Living the Mindful Life*. Boston: Shambhala Publications.

References

Beutler, L. E., B. Bongar, and J. N. Shurkin. 1998. *Am I Crazy, Or Is It My Shrink?* New York: Oxford University Press.

Cronkite, K. 1994. *On the Edge of Darkness: Conversations about Conquering Depression.* New York: Delta Trade Paperbacks.

The Dalai Lama. 2000. *Transforming the Mind: Teachings on Generating Compassion.* Translated by G. T. Jinpa. London: Thorsons.

Firestone, R. W. 1985. *The Fantasy Bond: Structure of Psychological Defenses.* Santa Barbara, Calif.: Glendon Association.

———. 1988. *Voice Therapy: A Psychotherapeutic Approach to Self-Destructive Behavior.* Santa Barbara, Calif.: Glendon Association.

———. 1990. *Compassionate Child-Rearing: An In-Depth Approach to Optimal Parenting.* Santa Barbara, Calif.: Glendon Association.

———. 1997a. *Combating Destructive Thought Processes: Voice Therapy and Separation Theory.* Thousand Oaks, Calif.: Sage.

———. 1997b. *Suicide and the Inner Voice: Risk Assessment, Treatment, and Case Management.* Thousand Oaks, Calif.: Sage.

Firestone, R. W., and J. Catlett. 1989. *Psychological Defenses in Everyday Life.* Santa Barbara, Calif.: Glendon Association.

———. 1999. *Fear of Intimacy*. Washington, D.C.: American Psychological Association.

Firestone, R. W., L. Firestone, and J. Catlett. 1997. *A Voice Therapy Training Manual*. Santa Barbara, Calif.: Glendon Association

Love, P., and S. Shulkin. 1997. *How to Ruin a Perfectly Good Relationship*. Austin, Tex.: Love and Shulkin.

McClure, L. 2000. *Anger and Conflict in the Workplace: Spot the Signs, Avoid the Trauma*. Manassas Park, Va.: Impact Publications.

Perris, C., L. Jaconsson, H. Lindström, L. vanKnorring, and H. Perris. 1980. Development of a new inventory for assessing memorites of parental rearing behavior. *Acta Psychiatrica Scandinavia* 61:265–278.

Robert W. Firestone, Ph.D., is a psychologist, author, and artist who was engaged in the private practice of psychotherapy from 1957 to 1979 working with a wide range of patients, expanding his original ideas on schizophrenia, and applying these concepts to a comprehensive theory of neurosis. In 1979, he joined the Glendon Association as its consulting theorist. Dr. Firestone's publications include *The Fantasy Bond, Compassionate Child-Rearing*, and *Fear of Intimacy*. His studies of negative thought processes led to the development of an innovative therapeutic methodology described in *Voice Therapy, Suicide and the Inner Voice, Combating Destructive Thought Processes,* and this book.

Lisa Firestone, Ph.D., is Program and Education Director of the Glendon Association, and adjunct faculty at the University of California, Santa Barbara. Since 1987, she has been involved in clinical training and applied research in the areas of suicide and violence. These studies resulted in the development of Firestone Assessment of Self-destructive Thoughts (FAST) and Firestone Assessment of Violent Thoughts (FAVT). Dr. Firestone's other publications include: *Voices in Suicide, Assessing Violent Thoughts: The Relationship Between Thought Processes and Violent Behavior, The Treatment of Sylvia Plath,* and *The Good Life: Sustaining Feeling, Passion and Meaning in a High-Tech Age.* She is an active presenter at national and international conferences in the areas of couple relations, voice therapy, and child abuse.

Joyce Catlett, M.A., is an author and lecturer who has collaborated with Dr. Robert Firestone in writing ten books, most recently coauthoring *Fear of Intimacy*. Since 1982, Ms. Catlett has been a lecturer and workshop facilitator and has coproduced thirty-seven video productions for the Glendon Association in the areas of parent-child relations, suicide, couple relations, and voice therapy. Ms. Catlett developed and trained instructors in the Compassionate Child-Rearing Parent Education Program.

Some Other
New Harbinger Titles

The End of-life Handbook, Item 5112 $15.95

The Mindfulness and Acceptance Workbook for Anxiety, Item 4993 $21.95

A Cancer Patient's Guide to Overcoming Depression and Anxiety, Item 5044 $19.95

Handbook of Clinical Psychopharmacology for Therapists, 5th edition, Item 5358 $55.95

Disarming the Narcissist, Item 5198 $14.95

The ABCs of Human Behavior, Item 5389 $49.95

Rage, Item 4627 $14.95

10 Simple Solutions to Chronic Pain, Item 4825 $12.95

The Estrogen-Depression Connection, Item 4832 $16.95

Helping Your Socially Vulnerable Child, Item 4580 $15.95

Life Planning for Adults with Developmental Disabilities, Item 4511 $19.95

Overcoming Fear of Heights, Item 4566 $14.95

Acceptance & Commitment Therapy for the Treatment of Post-Traumatic Stress Disorder & Trauma-Related Problems, Item 4726 $58.95

But I Didn't Mean That!, Item 4887 $14.95

Calming Your Anxious Mind, 2nd edition, Item 4870 $14.95

10 Simple Solutions for Building Self-Esteem, Item 4955 $12.95

The Dialectical Behavior Therapy Skills Workbook, Item 5136 $21.95

The Family Intervention Guide to Mental Illness, Item 5068 $17.95

Finding Life Beyond Trauma, Item 4979 $19.95

Five Good Minutes at Work, Item 4900 $14.95

It's So Hard to Love You, Item 4962 $14.95

Energy Tapping for Trauma, Item 5013 $17.95

Thoughts & Feelings, 3rd edition, Item 5105 $19.95

Transforming Depression, Item 4917 $12.95

Helping A Child with Nonverbal Learning Disorder, 2nd edition, Item 5266 $15.95

Leave Your Mind Behind, Item 5341 $14.95

Learning ACT, Item 4986 $44.95

ACT for Depression, Item 5099 $42.95

Integrative Treatment for Adult ADHD, Item 5211 $49.95

Freeing the Angry Mind, Item 4380 $14.95

Living Beyond Your Pain, Item 4097 $19.95

Call **toll free, 1-800-748-6273,** or log on to our online bookstore at **www.newharbinger.com** to order. Have your Visa or Mastercard number ready. Or send a check for the titles you want to New Harbinger Publications, Inc., 5674 Shattuck Ave., Oakland, CA 94609. Include $4.50 for the first book and 75¢ for each additional book, to cover shipping and handling. (California residents please include appropriate sales tax.) Allow two to five weeks for delivery.

Prices subject to change without notice.